God's Printer for Poland

God's Printer for Poland

Sharing God's Love in
Communist Eastern Europe—
A Modern Miracle from
One Man's Dream

Bill Kapitaniuk's Story
as told to
Halyna Smith

Larry Leuenberger, *Illustrator*

Foreword by Warren W. Wiersbe

BAKER BOOK HOUSE
Grand Rapids, Michigan 49516

Contents

Foreword

Although now I serve as honorary chairman, for more than ten years I served actively as Chairman of the Board of Slavic Gospel Association. What a privilege it was to minister with this group of dedicated Christians who are burdened to reach Slavic people around the world!

As I think back over our many business meetings, two things stand out in my mind. The first is the way we so often interrupt our business to spend time in prayer. The atmosphere is one of praise and prayer, and we go home feeling spiritually revived.

The second thing that stands out in my mind is the way one man's name kept cropping up—Bill Kapitaniuk. At one meeting, I jokingly said, "We have three items of business this evening: old business, new business, and Bill Kapitaniuk."

Not that Bill was creating problems for us, or that he was more important than any of our other fine missionaries. It's just that Bill was always discovering a new opportunity, or daring to try a new approach, or asking for our approval for an exciting new venture of faith. He seemed to be living in Hebrews 11 seven days a week!

I'm grateful that Halyna Smith has caught some of the miracle of the Kapitaniuks' ministry in the pages of this book. Halyna is not only a skillful writer, but she also has a keen understanding of the work of SGA and the challenge of reaching the Communist world with the gospel. I don't know of anybody better qualified to work with Bill and his family in putting this "faith testimony" together.

The Kapitaniuks would probably call themselves an "ordinary family," but God has done extraordinary things through them because they have dared to believe God. My prayer is that God will use this book to increase your faith, to burden your heart to pray and give so that Slavic peoples might be reached for Christ, and, if it is His will, to call you to give yourself to God for service somewhere in this needy world, starting right at home.

"But the people that do know their God shall be strong, and do exploits" (Daniel 11:32 KJV).

Fasten your safety belt! Here come the exploits!

Warren W. Wiersbe
Back to the Bible Broadcast
Lincoln, Nebraska 68501

Preface

Nearly ten years ago, I was one of about forty very excited, partially prepared, and somewhat apprehensive young people spending a final week of orientation in France before traveling into Eastern Europe. At one point I was blindfolded and led down a winding stairway into a musty smelling basement. When the blindfold was removed, I thought I'd been transported to an East European border; I was in a small, damp stone room facing a stern, uniformed, Slavic-looking man. A rickety wooden table and bare lightbulb were the only things separating me from his cold, unsmiling stare. During the few short minutes I sat shaking before this "official," trying to correctly answer the questions he fired at me, I discovered a new respect for the word *interrogation*. Later I learned that the "official" was our host, Bill Kapitaniuk.

I soon found that Bill was much more than a good actor. Even in the short time we had with him, he strongly impressed

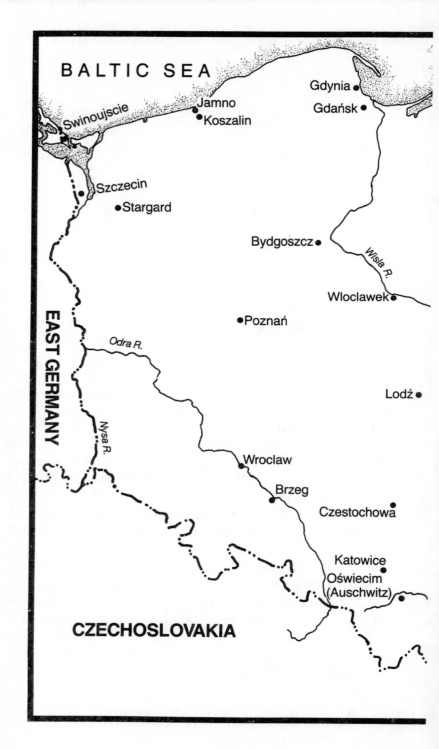

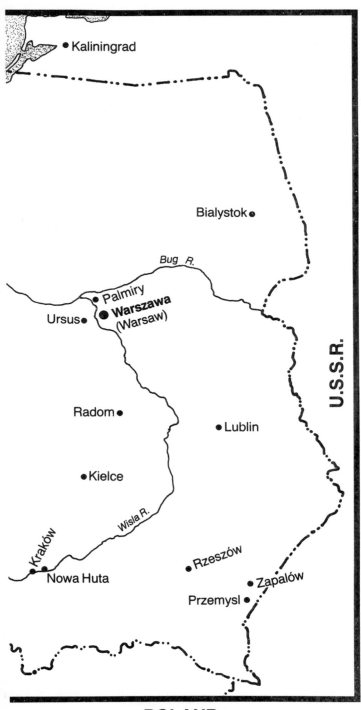

POLAND

me as a very godly man and an outstanding expositor of the Word of God. In addition, he had an inspiring way of challenging us with the tremendous needs in Eastern Europe.

Over the years I have developed a deep respect for Bill and his ongoing work and felt privileged when I was asked to write his biography. But how do you reduce a dynamic life to mere paper and ink? After several attempts, I decided the best way to recount Bill's life of determination and enthusiasm was to write as he told it to me—in the first person.

If, through this book, you see afresh what God can do with a life totally yielded to Him, if you are challenged that God does answer prayer and perform modern-day miracles, and if you catch a glimpse of how God can work even in areas that we may consider closed to the message of the gospel, I'll know that I have captured at least part of Bill's vision within these pages.

Halyna Smith

1

Soccer, Anyone?

This is illegal! You can't bring any ink into the country!" The Polish border official frowned at us, squaring his shoulders and thrusting out his jaw for emphasis. He couldn't have been more than twenty-three or twenty-four, but the khaki-colored uniform stiffly framed his boyish features, giving him an air of authority.

The late-evening sun of that mid-September day in 1984 was still quite warm. Was it only that morning that my brother-in-law George and I had been talking and laughing with my family around our breakfast table in northern France? Now we were on Poland's doorstep. Poland! That memorable country whose people had so intrigued and captured my heart when I had first visited there many years before. Despite the heat, my skin tingled with expectation. What treasure I brought this time! And in a quantity that would stagger the comprehension of my dear Polish friends.

Reluctantly, I turned my thoughts back to our present dilemma. For all her charm, Poland was also an avowedly communist nation. Since 1944 the government had maintained stringent rules for crossing its borders. Anything even remotely suspect of being "detrimental" to the Polish people—anything that seemed capable of undermining the country's communistic ideals—could be confiscated at whim. But *ink*? What could possibly be wrong with ink?

An interminable day of driving had taken its toll; George and I were dog-tired. We had covered over six hundred miles in only ten hours, and as we sat under the guard's scrutinizing gaze, I realized afresh that we were no longer young. What did this guard mean, no ink? I took my hand off the steering wheel and scratched my head, wondering what the problem could be. Though I had previously been detained at borders many times, possession of ink had never been the reason!

I looked up at the official and our eyes met and locked. His stare was cold, his face unflinching. Resolutely, I plunged ahead: "But there are only four cans. It's for a pastor."

"Do you have a permit for it?"

A permit? How were we to explain to the official that we never meant to be carrying this ink in the first place?

"No, we don't have a permit." Two nights before, in our scramble to load the Polish government truck with fifteen tons of *Illustrated New Testaments*, building materials and clothing, we had somehow overlooked the ink. This morning, as I was preparing to leave France, I had noticed it in a corner of the storage room, pushed aside in the shuffle. I remembered that a Polish friend of mine needed it very badly, so I had tossed it into the back of my car, not realizing that we would need a permit to bring it across the Polish border.

My eyes searched the border complex. Where was the pastor from Warsaw whom we had raced against the clock to meet? He was supposed to have the importation permit for our New Testaments. And, especially, where was the truck carrying those New Testaments? It should have been here by now; the

drivers and I had agreed to meet at 8:30 P.M. I forced my eyes back to the young official.

His face registered no emotion. "You can't bring any ink into the country without a permit. It's illegal."

I ran my hand through my hair and sighed. A long drive, no pastor, no permit, no New Testaments, and now this snag going through customs. I was tired, confused, frustrated. "But I didn't know—there must be some way. My friend, a pastor—he needs it badly. And it's only four cans!"

I sensed the official's blood churning as the color rushed to his cheeks. That we had no permit, along with my obvious frustration, seemed to agitate him. "No! It's not permitted." He paused, glared at me through squinted eyes, and added, "I think you'd better come with me." He opened the car door and motioned for me to step out.

With my thoughts racing, I followed him past an empty wooden bench and several cement columns. I was more annoyed than alarmed, for I knew from past experience that border delays could be costly in terms of time. What if the Polish pastor arrived now and couldn't find me? Would he recognize my car? Would he think I hadn't come? I began to pray silently. The Lord knew our situation and somehow would show us a way out of this.

We walked on to a gray stone building. Here the official stopped, opened the door, and gestured for me to precede him into the room.

A stocky, middle-aged official looked up from his desk as we entered. To me, his weathered face was a portrait of the varied climates he had had to face in his country's rugged history. Obviously bored with the paperwork strewn across his desk, he listened with interest to his young protégé's story. Then he turned to me and repeated the verdict I had already heard: we could not bring the ink with us into Poland.

Again I tried to explain why we had the ink and how necessary it was to our friend. I tried every line of reasoning I could think of, but nothing moved this official or his young subordinate. They flatly refused to let me into Poland with the ink. For two and a half hours we batted the issue back and forth.

At about 10:30 P.M., in the midst of our heated discussion, a Polish soldier rushed in.

"Kapitaniuk—is he here?"

"Yes," I replied.

"There's someone outside looking for you."

I hurried past the Polish officials, pushed open the door, and stood framed in the light from the office. I squinted as my eyes became accustomed to the darkness that had fallen during our "discussion." Then I smiled as I recognized the features of a pastor friend from Poznan. Although he was not the pastor from Warsaw whom I had been expecting, it was good to see a familiar face. Especially since this was the "friend" who needed the ink! I lunged at him, grabbing him up in a great bear hug and exclaiming, "Praise the Lord! I have your ink— but come in and explain to these guards that it's for you!" As we moved back toward the door, I noticed his wife standing in the shadows of a nearby cement column.

The three of us entered the building, and my Polish friends began to elaborate on their need for the ink. But the harder we tried to explain, the more irritated the guards became. They kept shaking their heads and asserting, "You *must* have a permit. You can't bring in any material for printing, because of Solidarity."

Of course! How could I have forgotten? The conflict between this budding workers' union and the Polish government had reached a peak during 1984 and was causing a mounting tension among Polish authorities. Officials were also becoming more and more upset with the amount of underground printed matter that Solidarity was producing. Hence, all printing materials were being strictly controlled at the borders because of the government's fear that they might end up in the wrong hands. Our ink situation was more serious than I had realized.

Just when our discussion seemed deadlocked, the middle-aged customs man suddenly looked up at the pastor and exclaimed, as if it were registering for the first time, "You come from Poznan?"

The pastor looked puzzled. "Yes."

The official scratched his chin and frowned slightly. "Next

Wednesday there's going to be a soccer match between the British team from Liverpool, England, and our Polish team. I believe the games are to be held in Poznan, aren't they?''

The pastor smiled. ''Yes, they are.''

Rising from his chair, the older official clasped his hands behind his back and slowly walked around his desk to where the pastor was seated. He stopped and peered into the pastor's face. ''You couldn't get us some tickets, could you?''

The pastor's smile widened. ''Yes, as a matter of fact I could. I have some friends at the ticket office. How many do you need?''

The official was also smiling now. ''Three.''

''No problem,'' the pastor assured him. ''I guarantee you three tickets if you'll let us take this ink with us.''

The official's smile vanished. Once again the room was charged with an almost tangible tension as silence descended. The younger customs man looked up from the declarations forms he had nearly completed—the forms stating that I was to leave the ink at the border. As I looked at the older official, I could almost see the wheels turning in his head. This was a serious matter, and he was training a younger official. If he gave in, what kind of respect would that young guard have for him? And what if the higher authorities found out that he had allowed ink to enter the country without a permit?

But I could also see that he—and the younger official—were desperately anxious to see that soccer match! The older guard ventured to look at his colleague, and the seconds seemed to drag by as the two men conversed with their eyes. Apprehension, frustration, and finally resignation passed between them in that look. Then the middle-aged official snatched up the declaration papers and studied them for several moments, scowling. Finally he turned to the Polish pastor. ''Okay,'' he growled as he began ripping up the forms. ''Take your ink and go!''

Without giving the officials a chance to change their minds, the pastor grabbed the ink and we headed out to our cars. I glanced at my watch: 11:00 P.M. We had been at the border for three hours. When George and I arrived at the next section of the border compound, we asked the officials about the Polish government truck carrying all our New Testaments and other goods, which should have been there two and a half hours before. "No," they said, "it hasn't arrived yet." The pastor from Warsaw, with the permit for the New Testaments, had not arrived either.

Well, at least we had our ink! But what about the truck and the permit? To my dismay, I then discovered that my friend from Poznan had been unable to contact the pastor in Warsaw as planned, to tell him when I would be at the border and needing the permit. That's why he had come to the border himself, to see if he could assist in some way.

Now what? How would the truck ever get our materials across the border without a permit? We decided to double-check at the PEKAES compound, the Polish government's international transportation station located just inside the Polish border. All government trucks that travel outside of Poland have to check in at this station as soon as they arrive back in the country. Perhaps, by some miracle, our truck would be there.

But the answer was the same: "No, that truck hasn't arrived from France yet." By now it was midnight. Because the truck had not arrived, and neither had the pastor with the permit, we felt that it was useless to stay at the border. George and I followed our friends to Poznan, and around 2:00 A.M. we fell into an exhausted sleep.

A few hours later I was jerked back to reality by a jangling phone. I could hear the pastor's voice in the next room, and soon there was a rap on my door. The pastor's face was beaming as he poked his head into my room. "That was customs. The truck has arrived in Poznan with the literature. They wanted to know if we could go and check it out."

The truck had arrived—and in Poznan! How could that be? Rubbing my eyes sleepily, I asked, "What time is it?"

"Eight o'clock."

I rolled out of bed and started dressing. "Well, we'd better see what the story is."

Standing in the kitchen, we thanked the Lord for the truck's safe arrival. Then the pastor and I gulped some coffee and left for the Poznan customs office. As we pulled into the customs area, I spotted the two Polish drivers of the PEKAES truck, whom I had met in France just four days earlier. We pulled our car alongside of them and I rolled down the window. "What happened?" I asked. "You were supposed to meet us at the border at eight-thirty last night."

One of the drivers shrugged. He was a husky man in his late thirties with sparse blond hair. "We just couldn't seem to get the truck going. We tried our best, but for some reason the motor was very sluggish. Those kilometers weren't decreasing and we couldn't get there as we promised you. In fact, we didn't arrive at the border until one A.M."

I was dumbfounded. How did the truck ever get through customs, when the clearance for its contents was still in Warsaw? "But how did you get through without any permit?"

The truck driver smiled, revealing a few shining gold teeth. "Well, when we arrived at the border, the customs men opened our truck. When they saw what we had, one of them wanted to put out an alarm and awaken the army to unload the whole truck right there at the border. But suddenly a young officer came along. He looked at my papers and said, 'No, let's seal the truck and let them go on to Poznan.'"

The sealing of the truck explained one thing: why the drivers had been allowed to bring the truck to Poznan. Once a vehicle is sealed, it cannot be opened until it reaches the point of destination indicated on the visa.

But several other questions remained unanswered. With an unlikely solution forming in my mind, I asked the truck drivers the name of the officer. When they replied, I smiled and shook my head in disbelief. "Well, praise the Lord!" The officer was one of the two men to whom we had promised tickets for the soccer match in Poznan!

Who would have guessed that the promise of three soccer tickets would allow us to import, in a Polish government truck, 27,000 *Illustrated New Testaments* in the Polish language? New Testaments that we had printed on our own press in France for the people of Poland? Elation, awe, gratefulness, and deep joy simultaneously overwhelmed me as I realized what the Lord was enabling us to do for Poland. The dreams that my heart had held for years were at last coming to fruition. Dreams that had begun to form after I had learned the Polish language and visited that country innumerable times. Dreams that were not without their share of pain, heartache, and frustration, but dreams that were also laced with the threads of miracle.

2

Eternal Soles

Bill, there's a letter for you!" My mother set aside the bowl of potatoes she was peeling and wiped her hands on her apron. She pulled a long envelope from her skirt pocket as the screen door banged behind me. Sighing and shaking her head, she reached across the kitchen table to hand me the letter. "That door is going to fall off its hinges one of these days!"

But I was only half listening. I had put in a hard morning's work out in the field. The sun had warmed considerably since dawn, and I was hot, tired, and hungry. A drop of sweat fell from my chin to the envelope as I looked at the return address. At last: the long-awaited application form from Prairie Bible Institute! I had two more years of high school to complete and wanted to do so in an atmosphere of Christian fellowship. I tore open the envelope and glanced over the questions.

Everything seemed to be in order. I returned the form to the envelope and stuffed it into my shirt pocket.

Dad, my brothers, and I enjoyed one of my mother's substantial lunches and then headed for the field again to spend our afternoon among the rows of half-grown wheat, oats, and barley. In the summertime, dusk came late to Evansburg, Alberta, so by evening we had worked a very full day. We were all exhausted when we returned to the house for supper.

After eating and the dishes were done, our family usually either gathered in the sitting room to listen to the radio or wandered out to the front porch to read a book or chat. That night, as everyone headed off to relax, I pulled up a chair at our old kitchen table and took the now-crumpled application form from my pocket. I unfolded it and began to answer the questions.

Name. Well, that was easy: Bill Kapitaniuk.

Date and place of birth. I thoughtfully chewed the eraser on my pencil. There was more behind this question than the simple answer I would give. I remembered the story well; my mother had told it to me many times. . . .

The year was 1928. My parents then lived in the Ukraine, where life had become increasingly difficult in the years since the communist revolution: "Unless you stole and lied, you'd just die of starvation!" My mother didn't see how she and my father could survive with more children than the two young sons they already had. Although she was devoutly religious in her Eastern Orthodox faith, she did away with several would-be brothers or sisters of mine before they were born.

As life became more and more unbearable, my father contrived a plan to leave the Ukraine and enter Poland. He would need money, of course, but he had that; he owned a substantial amount of livestock. The snag was that only one horse and one cow per person would be allowed to cross the border into Poland. So, to increase the assets that my dad could take along, he hired some Jewish ladies (who also wanted to leave the Ukraine) and had "Kapitaniuk" passports forged for them. When my parents, brothers, and the

Jewish women all arrived at the Polish border, there were no problems. Our "aunties" simply answered to the names of Mary and Anne Kapitaniuk!

Once in Poland, our Jewish "relatives" dispersed and my dad sold all the horses and cows. He then purchased tickets for himself, my mother, and my two brothers to sail for Canada. Very soon after their arrival, I had the privilege of coming into this world in Grosmont, Alberta. Though I had been conceived in the Ukraine, during some of the most difficult times that my mother faced, for some reason she had decided not to abort me. . . .

How did you become a Christian? Tell us a little about your early Christian growth and why you'd like to come to our high school. As I studied the application, my mind drifted back to my early days on our Canadian farm—160 acres of bush, hills, and rocks that my parents had bought as a homestead for a mere ten dollars. What a paradise that frontier farm had seemed to me as a young boy—just us and the wolves, the coyotes, and the wild game! It took me a long time to realize that my dad spent fifteen years of his life making eighty acres of that land fit to cultivate. Here was where I came to know the Lord, after my mother's striking conversion.

When I was eight years old, my mother went through a time of increased frustration and depression. Being an extremely religious person, she had an awareness of sin, but she could not find a way to shed her guilt. She had told me that before she left the Ukraine, she used to say to herself, "Here in the Soviet Union I can't live without sinning; unless I lie and steal, I'll starve to death. But the day I go to Canada, I will certainly be able to live the way God wants me to live."

My mother had thought that by merely changing countries her life would be completely new. But she failed to realize one thing: her "wicked heart" would be the same in Canada as it had been in the Ukraine. Her newfound political freedom did not bring the inner peace she had anticipated, and she found that lying and stealing came as easily in Canada as they had in the Ukraine. She wondered why. Surely here in freedom she ought to be able to live a godly life! She did not realize that outward circumstances could never satisfy the inner longings of her heart. After eight years, she was so overwhelmingly disillusioned that one day she left the house, not even knowing where she was going.

She hadn't walked very far when she heard singing coming from a house. "What kind of people are singing?" she wondered. "Why would anyone want to sing?" Her life was so miserable that she could scarcely imagine anyone doing such a thing. She had no song; nothing in her new life in Canada was going the way she had hoped it would.

The singing continued—beautiful singing. Something about it compelled my mother to stop. She stood listening. Finally her curiosity got the best of her and she walked up to the house and opened the door.

A group of simple-looking farm folk were gathered, singing hymns. My mother spotted an empty chair and sat down to listen. When the singing stopped, a middle-aged man in overalls and flannel shirt stood up. He began to preach with power and conviction, presenting the simple gospel message with clarity. My mother had never before heard the gospel conveyed like this and was quite taken up with what he had to say. One thing in particular really grabbed her attention. The preacher had paused in his presentation and had begun earnestly searching the faces of those gathered. As he did so, he remarked, "I have such peace and joy in my heart; I wouldn't exchange my life with anybody's for a million dollars!"

My mother began to turn his statement over in her mind. "Where does he find this peace and joy?" she wondered. "I've been searching for it for forty years and haven't found it!" This one sentence so intrigued her that she asked when the next meeting would be and returned the following Sunday.

The same man was preaching again, this time about the prodigal son. At the conclusion of his message, he looked out over the congregation and asked, "Is there anyone here like the prodigal son? Would you like to come back to God? You raise your hand, and I'll pray for you."

The preacher's words reached deep into my mother's heart and touched a responsive chord. She realized that she needed the prayers of that preacher. But as she cast a furtive glance around the room, she recognized a neighbor. She was too embarrassed to raise her hand.

But she was also in a very desperate state. She *had* to see if she could really know that same peace and joy that the preacher had spoken of before. As quickly and inconspicuously as she could, my mother raised not a hand, but a finger. Surely her neighbor wouldn't notice that!

But the Lord saw her finger, stretched upwards in feeble but hopeful faith. Suddenly my mother fell on her knees and began to weep. "I didn't see anybody after that," she told me later, "only a holy God before me, a sinful woman. I felt so unclean in the face of such holiness. It was then I knew I deserved only death and hell." With trembling, she began to confess her sin before the Lord. And then an amazing thing happened: she felt as if a big stone had rolled off her soul, as if the Lord had opened up the heavens and filled her entire being with the glory of God! The change was so dramatic that she later remarked, "I wasn't walking on earth anymore; I was flying!"

Late that night, when Mother arrived home after the meeting, she burst into the house saying, "Boys! Come outside! Look! There are wonderful lights in the sky!" We rushed outside, but couldn't see any lights. Disappointed, she shared with us what had happened: As she was returning home from the service, she had to cross a muskeg full of mud and water. The only way across was a pathway made of logs. Before she reached the bog, she began to wonder just how she would get across it. The night was pitch-black and she would never be able to see her way. Then, just as she arrived at the foot of the log pathway, a huge light appeared in the sky. What had been complete darkness now seemed as bright as noon! My mother crossed the muskeg with no difficulty, and the light was there in the sky until she reached home. She had rushed in to share this with us, but when we went outside, the light was gone.

From that day on, our mother was a different woman. And every day she began to tell us that we, too, needed to accept Jesus Christ as our personal Savior. At first we didn't know what to think of her; we couldn't understand what she was talking to us about because it was the first time we had ever heard the gospel. We thought that maybe she was going through a phase in one of her depressions, except she seemed to be so very happy. That first night I remember talking with my brothers as we lay in bed; we decided we would wait until morning to see if she wouldn't change after a good sleep! But that very next morning, before we went to school, she preached to us again about Jesus. This went on for about six months; every day, every time she had an opportunity, she would talk to us about Jesus.

One evening in the middle of winter, we heard a knock on the door. A white-haired old man stood there; as soon as we opened the door he walked in and exclaimed, "Praise the Lord!" At that, my brother Cosmo left the room in disgust, muttering, "It's not enough that Mother preaches to us night and day; now this stranger arrives and the first thing he tells us is 'Praise the Lord!'"

This man, Mr. Kucher, was about sixty-five years old and was also from the Soviet Union. He had heard that my mother had been converted and had walked twenty-five miles to see her. He and my mother had some terrific times of Christian fellowship during the length of his stay.

The morning after Mr. Kucher arrived, my brothers and I got up, had breakfast, and were about ready to leave for school when he stopped us. "Boys," he began, "before you go to school, I'd like to pray with you." Well, to be polite, we stayed behind. Brother Kucher took his Bible and began to read aloud the story of Christ's crucifixion. I can still see him sitting by our table in that log cabin, reading with tears streaming down his cheeks. Then he looked up at us and said, "Boys, Jesus died for you, too. Would you like to accept Him into your hearts? Let's pray!"

So we all knelt down around the table, and my brothers and I prayed for salvation. I prayed a very simple prayer: "Lord, I'm a sinner; forgive me and come into my heart." When I walked outside, I thought the world had changed: The sky seemed bluer, the horizon seemed clearer—even the snow seemed whiter! Why did everything look so much better? Of course, the world hadn't changed at all; Jesus Christ had penetrated my young heart.

My brothers and I rushed off to school because it was late. We shared with the other children what had happened to us that morning, but soon we didn't have any more friends at school. The majority of Ukrainian immigrants to Canada continued in the Eastern Orthodox faith in which they had been raised and often had a hard time understanding anyone who was different. Our classmates began to call us "Shtundists," a nickname they gave to people like us who left the Orthodox religion and went to the evangelical churches. But we didn't mind. We continued to witness to those children in spite of the fact that they often harassed us.

Once we three boys were converted, my mother enlisted our prayers for our father's conversion. From the time she had come to faith in Jesus, she had been speaking to him about the Lord but to no apparent avail. Our dad was Eastern Orthodox, but he knew nothing of a personal faith in Jesus Christ. To him, religion meant allegiance to a specific church, and my mother had changed her allegiance. He insisted, "The religion I was born in is the religion I will die in!" Still, my mother persevered, all the while knowing that my brothers and I were praying, too.

One morning she just ran out of patience; my brothers and I came downstairs for breakfast to find her in her bedroom on her knees, praying. Hearing us at the doorway, she looked up and declared, "Boys, I've made up my mind. I'm not going to work; I'm not going to eat. I'm going to stay on my knees and pray until your father's converted." So, we made our own

breakfast that morning and went off to school wondering what would happen.

Late that afternoon we hurried home, and Mother met us at the door, her face wreathed in smiles. "Boys," she began, "your father has also entered into the family of God!" Then she and my dad proceeded to tell us how it had happened.

Our father had been very restless all that morning. He had left the house to do the chores, thinking that perhaps if he busied himself, his inner turmoil would cease.

But, as he fed the cows and pitched the hay, his mind was spinning. Again and again he would hear my mother's voice speaking to him of Jesus and quoting passages of Scripture. Or he would see afresh the tenderness, the joy, and the peace that she had now. And all the while a nagging ache in his heart reminded him that he was not at peace, that he had no real joy. An inner battle raged within him, one side compelling him to turn his life over to God, the other trying desperately to convince him that he was doing just fine as he was.

On this day, for some reason, nothing would ease the aching, and nothing would calm the raging battle in his soul. The more he tried not to think about Jesus, the more thoughts of the Lord would flash across his mind, leaving unanswered questions in their wake. As he explained it, he felt like a prisoner inside his own body; he could not escape.

By eleven that morning, mentally, emotionally, and spiritually exhausted, Dad could bear the tension no longer. At last he realized that he had to do something about this Jesus whom his wife spoke about with her every waking breath. With a sigh, he walked back to the house and began to look for her.

He was unprepared for what he found. My mother was kneeling at their bed, her back to him. He heard her begging, pleading with God to do something drastic, to bring someone she dearly loved to Himself. As Dad listened, he realized with a pang that she was begging and pleading for him. A tear trickled down his cheek; then he began to sob uncontrollably. For so long he had resisted, but he could resist no longer. Kneeling next to my mother, he asked the Lord for forgiveness and new life.

Some months afterward, our entire family was baptized in a small lake in the woods, not far from our home town of Athabasca. Many of our neighbors came to watch, some out of curiosity, others out of genuine interest, and many to make fun of us. Some were so agitated by what they perceived as rejection of their Orthodox faith and alignment with the evangelicals that they threw horse manure into the water. We were the only evangelical Christian family in our area, and people wondered what had happened to us.

From Athabasca we moved to Evansburg. I went to high school there, and after classes I would often pull out my Bible, and the kids would come around and question me. Sometimes we gathered on a street corner, sometimes in a shop, often spending hours discussing their questions. Some of the ques-

tions were from those who were honestly searching for an-
swers, but many times the questions were posed to try to trick
me. Regardless of the motives for those sessions, through them
I came to be known as "Bible Bill."

As I began to grow in my Christian life, I was increasingly
aware of my lack of Christian fellowship. The attitude of the
kids toward God and the immorality in the high school
disturbed me very much, and I longed for Christian friends.
After finishing tenth grade, I decided I would quit school
unless I could go to a Christian one. This was why I was
applying to the high school at Prairie Bible Institute.

It was after 10:00 P.M. when I finally put down my pencil.
Then I quickly addressed an envelope, folded the application,
and shoved it inside.

The sitting room was empty as I walked over to my
mother's small wooden desk and took a stamp from the
cut-glass bowl. I licked the stamp and pressed it to the
envelope with my thumb. Then I grabbed my jacket from a
peg on the wall and stepped out onto the front porch. The
night was still and quiet except for the melodic chirping of the
crickets. I began the trek down our long, dusty driveway to the
mailbox. The postman wouldn't know to stop unless I raised
the red flag. . . .

"You mean you're not going?" Several weeks had passed,
and I squinted as the mid-afternoon sun danced behind Nick
Pasechnick's face. The church had been hot, even for August,
and it was good to get outside where the air at least was
moving.

Nick chewed thoughtfully on a blade of grass. "Well, not to
Prairie. I've changed my mind; I'm going to the Ukrainian
Bible School in Saskatoon."

I whistled with surprise and shook my head. Nick had
applied to Prairie just as I had, had been accepted, and had
made plans to go. Now, with a week left before classes were
due to begin, he had decided against Prairie and in favor of the

Bible school in Saskatoon. How did some people get all the breaks? Just a week earlier I had received a letter from Prairie saying that they had no room for me.

Suddenly, an idea hit me. If Nick didn't go to Prairie, that meant there would be a vacant spot. And if I arrived at the last minute, with all my suitcases—

"Nick, do they know at Prairie that you've changed your mind?"

"No, they still think I'm coming."

The cool office with its beige cement walls was a welcome relief after the hot, stuffy buses I had taken from home to Three Hills, Alberta. My suitcases were stacked in the hallway outside, awaiting what I was sure would be a simple registration procedure. I stood twisting my cap in my hands, wondering just what Miss Dearing was hunting for in those papers. I was confident; there was simple logic in my presence there in the principal's office at Prairie Bible Institute. But several minutes had passed already, and I was becoming impatient.

Miss Dearing was studying my application papers, and she also had a book that she seemed to be comparing with the papers. She frowned as she shuffled them. Finally, she looked up at me and stated very matter-of-factly, "Mr. Kapitaniuk, we have written that we have no room for you."

"Well," I began, "I'm sorry, but I have come to take the place of Nick Pasechnick. He was accepted, but he's not coming. So, I've come instead."

She tried to hide a smile. "This really isn't our normal procedure."

Was she stalling or was she serious? I had come so far; how could they not take me now? Her eyes looked so kind. But her jaw was set. Yes, she was serious. I stated my case: "But if Nick's not coming, you have one more space. And classes start in just a few days. I want so much to study here! In my application, didn't I mention how few Christians are in our area? How much I want and need Christian friends and some good Bible teaching?"

Miss Dearing quickly looked down at her papers again. She seemed flustered, even embarrassed. "I'll have to discuss this with the dean; I don't have the authority to accept you right here on the spot."

Later that day, dusk was falling as I started to walk from the high-school dorm toward the cafeteria. I smiled to think that I was actually here, at Prairie. The Lord had heard my prayer and given me my heart's desire. I would not fully comprehend for some time that I had put Prairie's administration in a real bind. Miss Dearing had discussed my situation with the dean and the president, but what could they do? I was there, bodily, to plead my case. I had all my suitcases with me, and classes were due to begin. And so, against their regular principles and procedures, they took me in.

One more thumbtack should do it, I thought. There! I stood back from the bulletin board to admire my handiwork. The bright kelly-green sign with the bold black letters really stood out from the majority of tiny ads typed or handwritten on 3" x 5" white index cards: SURE-GRIP, NON-SKID ETERNAL SOLES, GUARANTEED FOR 10,000 MILES. That ought to bring me some business!

I dearly loved my six years at Prairie Bible Institute; I was able to complete my last two years of high school and went on to take four years of Bible school. It seemed like seventh heaven after the previous dearth of Christian fellowship. But life was by no means easy. I had to study hard, and finances were tight. There were times when I didn't even have enough money for the postage stamp for a letter to my parents. So, I had tried to think of some ways to earn extra money. One idea that I thought would work was that of using old tires to repair boots. The tires wouldn't cost me a cent, and I could cut them up and use them for soles on work boots: "Eternal soles."

I was flooded with jobs and began to spend my entire Saturdays, from morning till night, cutting up tires and nailing those tire soles to work boots. After some time I began to have requests for thinner soles, so I ordered some regular soles from a shoe store.

One morning I received a note in my mailbox from Mr. Maxwell, the president of Prairie: "Please drop by and see me as soon as possible." I raised my eyebrows in surprise. This was strange. Why would Mr. Maxwell want to see me?

His secretary looked up from her typing as I poked my head into her office. "Oh, hi, Bill! Mr. Maxwell's been expecting you. Just a minute and I'll see if he's free to see you now." After a quick rap on the door and a few words with him, she turned around and motioned for me to come. "He's on the phone, but he'll just be a minute. Please be seated."

After a moment, Mr. Maxwell hung up the receiver and looked at me for a few seconds, not saying a word. He picked up a box from behind his chair and placed it on the desk in front of him. "Bill, come over here for a moment, would you? Do you know anything about this?"

The box had been opened, and Mr. Maxwell pulled back the flaps so that I could see the contents. Shoe soles, dozens of thin, black, rubber ones. I turned back one of the box flaps so I could see the return address. Then I looked at Mr. Maxwell. "Yes, sir, these are some shoe soles that I ordered. But how—?"

Mr. Maxwell frowned. "That *you* ordered?"

"Yes, sir. To earn a little extra money, I've been resoling work boots. I had been using old tires, but I started getting requests for thinner soles, so I ordered these." I paused and scratched my head. "But how did you—?"

Mr. Maxwell chuckled. "Resoling old work boots, eh? Well, Bill, I'm afraid the cobbler downtown is a bit concerned about the competition."

"Sir?"

"These soles arrived at the cobbler's shop in Three Hills. Apparently the company you ordered them from thought there was some mistake. They didn't think that anyone at Prairie Bible Institute would be needing a box of shoe soles, so they delivered them to the cobbler instead. He's a little upset that you're taking some of his business." He paused a moment and shook his head. "I'm afraid you'll have to give up shoe repair, Bill. We're a nonprofit organization and have no right to do business on our premises."

The auditorium was a maze of human bodies—laughing, talking, pushing slowly toward the exits. Chapel had just finished, and everyone was in a rush to leave. But I observed all this as if I were not really part of the pulsating throng. From the corner of my eye, I noticed what was happening, but my mind was far away, mulling over the closing words of our guest speaker.

I had heard of Peter Deyneka but was not prepared for him. When he stepped up to the platform, he looked very much like our typical chapel speakers. But the minute he opened his mouth, I was caught up in his magnetic fervor. His words packed a wallop that few could rival, urging us to pray and to evangelize. Even his broken English could not dilute his dynamism, his deep concern for those who did not know his Lord.

But the clincher for me was his closing request—a challenge to help evangelize the thousands of Slavic people who were in Europe's displaced persons camps. World War II had not only left them destitute—homeless, jobless, and penniless—but also without spiritual resources upon which to draw. Because of their desperate state, they were hungry to hear of a God who loved them and cared about what happened to them. The immediate opportunities for evangelization were phenomenal! "I'm sure," Mr. Deyneka said in closing, "that the Lord will speak to some of you about taking the gospel to these needy Slavic people."

My mind was reeling. How often at Prairie had I been challenged to share my faith in needy areas! Every time I heard a missionary from a foreign country, I responded, "Lord, I'd like to go there!" For a while, I wanted to go to South America because of the great need. Then I planned to go to Africa because the need there was also great. Right before Mr. Deyneka arrived, I had been planning to go to China to spread the gospel. And now this—a chance to work among my own Slavic people.

Little by little, my jumbled thoughts began to gel. I knew the language and I had the background. The thought of sharing my faith among Slavic people began to excite me. Why, I could begin work immediately without spending time studying languages and culture! I would need to pray more about it, but this seemed to me the perfect direction to take. Little did I know it then, but the stage was being set for a unique work in Eastern Europe. The backdrop for my dream had its first splash of paint.

3

"If I Speak with the Tongues of Men—and of English . . ."

The late-morning sun beat down on my neck as I headed my dad's tractor toward the red dot on the horizon that I knew to be the barn. Usually I loved the feel of the farm machinery in my hands, with the blue Canadian sky overhead and the rich brown earth beneath my feet. In early springtime, after the long rugged winter, the feeling was even more intense because it was so good to be outdoors at last! But today the joy was gone, and I sensed instead the restlessness that had become my recent companion. I sighed and wiped my forehead with the sleeve of my jacket.

As I drove through the open fields, my mind wandered from one thing to another. But my thoughts kept returning to one verse of a passage in Malachi that I had read that morning: " 'But cursed be the swindler who has a male in his flock, and vows it, but sacrifices a blemished animal to the Lord, for I am

a great King,' says the LORD of hosts, 'and My name is feared
among the nations' '' (Mal. 1:14).

Funny, I couldn't remember having seen that verse before.
Why did it keep repeating itself over and over in my mind, like
a phonograph record that keeps playing at the point where the
needle is stuck? There was something about it that I couldn't
quite put my finger on.

The red dot on the horizon was beginning to get larger. I
smiled as I gazed around at acre after acre of newly plowed soil.
Soon the green sprouts would poke their heads above the
ground and the spring phase of our work would begin. It was
a work that satisfied me to my very core. I belonged here in
this vast expanse of space and earth, doing what I loved to
do—didn't I? The vague uneasiness that had lately begun to
gnaw within me made me wonder if I was trying to convince
myself of something that could never be. But it seemed so
logical. And, besides, now that my parents were getting older,
they really needed me to help them keep the farm going.
Hadn't I come to a decision last week when mother and I had
had that conversation?

"A missionary?" My mother looked up from her knitting and eyed
me thoughtfully. "That's a fine idea, Bill, but you'd better think it over
carefully before you decide." She paused long enough to smooth the
little dress she was making. "You know, your father and I aren't
getting any younger. Dad really needs someone here to help him
work the farm. He doesn't have anyone else now."

Well, I had expected that line of reasoning from her. After all,
because I was the youngest, my mother would find it hardest to let go
of me. My two older brothers were already married and gone. And
here I was, alone with my parents.

But Slavic Gospel Association had already accepted me as a
missionary, and I wasn't asking my mother for alternatives. I had
simply told her that I was going to be a missionary to Europe. A
feeling of guilt seeped into my consciousness. Was I being selfish to
leave full responsibility of the farm to my aging parents in order to
take the gospel to Slavic refugees in Europe? Perhaps my mother

was right: perhaps I *should* think about my decision more thoroughly. Maybe there was a compromise.

As if she were reading my thoughts, my mother added, "Why don't you stay on the farm, grow wheat, and use the money you make selling it to support other missionaries?"

Now, *that* was an idea! Farming was in my blood, and I couldn't conceive of life without it. By this point in his career, my father had all the latest in farming machinery—huge tractors, a self-propelled combine, massive trucks. How I enjoyed driving them all! Maybe God *did* want me to remain a farmer and support other missionaries with the proceeds.

Suddenly I winced as if I'd been slapped. My restlessness, the reverberating verse, the snatch of conversation with my mother—somehow, between them, they had loosened a memory from the depths of my mind, the memory of a story my mother had once told me in rich detail. As it surfaced again, I realized why I had been so uneasy for the last several days. . . .

My mother paused briefly in the doorway of the small Orthodox church as her eyes adjusted to the darkness. Most of the people in the Ukrainian village where she lived were hard at work, but she had something special she had to do. The scent of incense from the morning service lingered, and my mother smiled as the shaft of light from the doorway glinted on the gilt of several icons. She reached up to adjust the kerchief on her head and entered the building, passing a column on which the creation story was depicted by a fourteenth-century artist. From another column the unsmiling faces of St. Athanasius, St. Agnes, and St. Ambrose greeted her. A few candles glimmered before the icon of St. Peter, and here she kneeled on the cold stone floor, crossed herself, and kissed the icon before she walked further.

When she reached the heavily ornamented icon of the Madonna and Child, she stopped. She groped in her apron pocket for the two-kopek piece she had brought with her and dropped it into a wooden box on a nearby table. Then she picked up a long, thin candle from another box, crossed herself before the icon and gazed for a moment at the two faces.

The features of Mother and Child were so darkened from the smoke of centuries of candles as to be barely recognizable. And the gold leaf that framed the faces was a striking contrast, gleaming every so often as it caught the light of the dozens of candles flickering on a stand in front of the icon. My mother lit her candle, and her arm shook as she placed it on the stand. "Dear God," she whispered, "may this child I'm carrying be totally Yours. I give him to You now, for Your service."

As I recalled my mother's story, the tractor seat bounced uncomfortably, but I hardly noticed. For I was the child my mother had been carrying. Before she left the Ukraine, when I was still within her womb, I had been promised to the Lord. And I remembered that this was by no means the only prayer she had offered on my behalf. After her conversion, my mother's supreme prayer was, "Lord, save Bill and make him a missionary."

Cursed be the swindler who has a male in his flock, and vows it, but sacrifices a blemished animal to the Lord. . . . Had I not been vowed to the Lord even before I was born? And then again after my mother's conversion? Somehow the money I would get selling wheat seemed "a blemished animal" compared to the life—*my* life—which had been promised to God.

Cursed be the swindler . . . cursed be the swindler . . . cursed be the swindler. . . . The words echoed relentlessly. No hint of compromise allowed here. The penalty for disobedience was a curse, and the curse would be on my mother! I shook my head, realizing that I could do nothing less than what the Lord expected. I only hoped my mother would understand.

As the tractor churned to a halt, I tried to formulate in my mind what I was going to say. I could picture my mother in the kitchen, putting the finishing touches on lunch. I glanced at the yard; there was no sign of my father's truck. Yes, now would be a good time to talk to her.

The screen door gave its usual squeak, and my mother looked up from the salad she was tossing. She smiled and nodded at the stove. "Give that gravy a stir, would you, Bill? It started boiling sooner than I thought it would."

"Mom," I began, "I need to talk to you about something."

"In a minute, Bill, as soon as I finish getting this ready for the table."

"I really need to talk to you now, Mom."

"I'm just about finished. One more little. . . ."

"Mom!"

Detecting the note of urgency in my voice, she dried her hands on the towel that had been lying on the counter. She gave me a wry smile and said, "I should know better than to try to keep you waiting when you've got something on your mind. What is it, Bill?"

I picked up the large black family Bible from my father's place at the table and turned to the Book of Malachi. My mother was next to me now, peering at the yellowed paper, worn around the edges with use. When I found the fourteenth verse of the first chapter, I held my finger under it and said, "Read this."

She read in silence, and when she looked up, her face was puzzled. "Curses, flocks, blemished animals—what does it mean?"

I set the Bible on the table and placed my hands on my mother's shoulders. "Mother," I said gently, "do you remember the story you told me of how, before you left the Ukraine, you prayed that I would be given into God's service—before I was even born?"

She nodded. A flash of comprehension passed across her face, and her lower lip began to quiver.

I continued: "And how you prayed for me, after you were converted and we were living here in Canada, that the Lord would save me and make me a missionary?"

Again she nodded. She turned her eyes toward the floor and a tear spilled down her cheek.

I pulled her close. "Mother, I must go to Europe with SGA. You promised me to the Lord, and I don't want His curse to fall on you if I stay here." A wan smile spread across her tear-filled face and she nodded. Softly I added, "I'm sure the Lord will bless you if you keep your promise."

Beads of sweat formed on my forehead as I leaned all my body's weight against the wall and pushed. Nothing happened. Well, I'd gone over every inch of this room and hadn't found any secret hiding place. It must be somewhere else.

The year was 1952. About fifteen months had passed since I had shown my mother that passage in Malachi. I had spent most of that time traveling with Peter Deyneka on a tour across America, speaking in meetings and raising my needed $120-per-month support. Now I was finally in Germany, ready to begin work in the displaced persons (D.P.) camps.

SGA had been given an old house in Augsburg, and, shortly after my arrival, my co-workers told me that somewhere in the house was a hidden chamber where food was kept during the war. I was determined to find that room but had been unsuccessful thus far.

The dust in the next room must have been an inch thick, and cobwebs connected lamps and furniture with the walls and ceiling. I pushed everything aside, groping behind old bookcases, chairs, and tables for a sliding wall panel, or perhaps an indentation in a baseboard.

I had nearly finished my search when my fingers ran across an odd bump in the wall. My heart pounding, I shoved some of the furniture away from the wall. I began to experiment, trying to push, slide, and pull the wall. Suddenly as I was pulling, the entire wall began to move and I was able to lift it almost effortlessly. The secret chamber at last!

As I crept in, I discovered a ham still hanging—a ham that must have been there for the last three years. It was covered with mold, but I took it outside and brushed and cleaned it until no mold remained. As we cut the ham, we looked it over carefully for spoilage and could find only one spot inside by the bone that was spoiled. A nearly perfect ham! I used it to cook some borsch, which we feasted on the whole week. My adventures in Europe had begun. . . .

The train jostled along as I rode in silence. Four months had passed since my arrival in Germany, and I had found a deep joy in sharing my faith with refugees from all over Eastern Europe. Sometimes it was with families, sometimes with individuals, and often with large groups. Mr. Deyneka had been right: these people who had lost everything were ripe to receive the gospel. Most of them arrived at the D.P. camps with few, if any, personal belongings and appreciated any material or spiritual help that we could give. Day after day, in helping these people, I experienced a contentment and satisfaction that I had never known before. I had not realized that something other than farming could give me fulfillment. But directing others to a personal faith in Jesus Christ brought a peace, a contentment, and a joy that farming could never match.

As the mountains and lush countryside sped past my window, I pulled Mr. Deyneka's letter out of my pocket and reread it for the third time that day: "A church in Belgium desperately needs help. The pastor passed away, and the church especially needs somebody to work with the young people. Could you go there?" The letter had arrived a few days before, and I had quickly gathered my belongings and caught a train to Belgium.

The church that the letter mentioned was made up of mainly Polish immigrants. Since it was located in the French-speaking section of Belgium, the members spoke both French and Polish. I had studied a little French back home in Athabasca, but only for a few months. I had found it difficult and time-consuming. All I could remember was *"Frère Jacques, frère Jacques, dormez-vous?"* And I knew no Polish. But since Mr. Deyneka would not have written if the need had not been pressing, I had agreed to go. . . .

A ripple of subdued chuckles passed through the congregation as I paused. I looked down at the huge pulpit Bible and smiled as I realized that I had done it once again. You would think that after nearly three years of almost constant practice I would have mastered the Polish language. But no. I had been trying to quote from First Corinthians 13 and had confused the words for "angel" and "English"—again. They were so similar in Polish that I often forgot which was which. And so, my rendering of First Corinthians 13:1 had come out, "If I speak with the tongues of men and of English. . . ."

In spite of the language difficulties and my youth (I was twenty-four when I arrived), the Lord had blessed my time in Liège, Belgium. The church had grown both spiritually and in numbers; we had baptized ten to twelve people every year. After three years, our meeting place was too small, so we began to build a much larger building. I was excited to learn how to lay bricks; in Canada most building was done with wood.

Officially I had been asked to come to Belgium as an assistant, to work with the youth. But the pastor who had died had served as the church's pastor, youth worker, and general spiritual leader; the congregation needed someone to carry on all these responsibilities. So, I became a sort of unofficial pastor, preaching at both services as well as working with the young people. Although I had neither the authority nor title of "pastor," I gained valuable experience as I took on more and more pastoral duties. I grew quite fond of the hard-working Polish-French folk in the congregation; they, in turn, grew fond of me and appreciated the help that I tried my best to give. My fluency in Polish and French grew as I used both almost constantly, and I learned much about Polish culture.

During the period before I arrived, another mission had helped the church financially and—partly because of that mission's involvement—my status was that of youth worker and not official pastor. When the congregation decided to build a new church building, this other mission provided the finances. Construction was well under way when the deacons of the congregation and leaders from this mission met to discuss the election of a pastor. A list of three candidates was compiled: two young men who were members of the other mission, and I, a member of Slavic Gospel Association.

At a special church meeting, the fifty members voted. When the votes were tallied, forty-five were for me. But when the deacons presented this decision to the other mission, their members would not accept it. They met with the deacons and said that I could not be the pastor for two reasons: first, because someone from their mission should be pastor, since they had invested so much in the church financially; and second because they would not provide the funds to finish the

new building if I were allowed to stay—and the church still
needed about $10,000.

Now the church had to determine whether, in light of these
circumstances, they still wanted me as their pastor. A vote was
taken, and the deacons decided to go along with the wishes of
the other mission. More than half of the church members were
not happy with this decision and left the church en masse,
without even finishing the meeting! These thirty people felt
that the others were choosing the $10,000 for their "spiritual
leader," instead of me.

The members of this splinter group asked me to be their
pastor. At first I did not accept, because that would mean I was
approving the split. But, after praying about it for a week, I felt
that I could not abandon these people; most of them were
converts from my three years in Liège. So I met with them and
said that if I came to help in their services, it would be for the
sole purpose of reuniting with the other congregation. And so,
for a year, the splinter group and I worked together with the
goal of getting back together with their brothers and sisters.

Of course, by the time news of all this had reached SGA
headquarters in America, my reputation (and therefore SGA's)
was hardly sacrosanct. I had become "the SGA missionary
who was splitting churches across Europe," and a very un-
happy SGA leadership recalled me to America. Against my
wishes, I returned home.

Disillusioned, hurt, and frustrated, I began to contemplate
my last three years. Though I had found real satisfaction in
evangelizing and pastoring, I wondered whether the misunderstandings, the heartaches, and the disappointments were
worth it. Did I have something to show for the time I had
invested—something I could share with supporting churches
and individuals?

As I reflected, I realized that, despite the difficulties, the
time spent in Europe was very special to me. I had seen God
work as I never had before and had especially grown to love
the Polish-French people with whom I had worked in Belgium.

Unbeknownst to me, the backdrop for my future dream—including evangelizing refugees, learning French and Polish, and pastoring a church—was nearly complete. Only the final touch was lacking.

4

Sophie's Choice

The noonday sun filtered down through the trees, forming a patchwork pattern on the ground below. Small groups of people clustered around the old white church building, laughing and talking and thinking about their Sunday dinners. Children played tag among their parents' coattails or skipped stones in the nearby stream.

"Sophie!" A middle-aged woman in a dark floral dress and a black felt hat smiled and waved her hand high in the air. "Sophie! I need to talk to you!"

Shielding her eyes from the sun, a slight, golden-haired young woman turned in the direction of the voice and began to dodge groups of people as she made her way toward the steadily bobbing black hat. Snatches of Polish, Russian, and Ukrainian filtered through the groups till at last she was face to face with the pastor's wife.

"Sophie!" A face wreathed in smiles and with kindly eyes peered out from under the rim of the black hat. "The Lord has put something very special on my heart for you!" She grasped Sophie's extended hand in both of hers.

Something special? Sophie smiled shyly. She could certainly do with some happy news. The last few months had been very difficult for her. For four years she had lived in Montreal, Canada, hoping that the change of air would relieve the headaches that had plagued her ever since a childhood accident in her native France. But her headaches were no better, and recently she had passed through some difficulties in the Bible school she was attending. A series of misunderstandings both there and at church, including being accused of something she had not done, had left an emptiness, an ache, and the seeds of bitterness in her heart. Why, she would never dream of doing the thing of which she had been accused! That anyone could think she could devastated her, and as a result she harbored a deep-seated resentment. She was tired of problems, of being misunderstood, of life in general. Just the attitude of the pastor's wife was soothing.

"Sophie, the Lord has put on my heart that one day you will be working with Polish people!" The pastor's wife beamed.

Sophie's smile disappeared and she stared in disbelief. This was the *special* news? To work with *Polish* people? All her life she had tried to forget her Polish ancestry. Although she had been born in France, Sophie's parents had come from Poland, and Sophie had learned Polish as her first language. Children can be cruel and Sophie had grown up with "Polack! Why don't you go back to your country?" ringing in her ears. The memories still hurt. No, she could never work with Polish people; she was *French*! An anger that had been festering for a long, long time surfaced as she shook her hand free from the firm grasp of the pastor's wife. Sophie's eyes were flaming now; she edged away and shook her head vehemently. "No! Never!"

The pastor's wife gave a little gasp. "But, Sophie! I thought you'd be pleased!"

"I'm sorry. But I'll *never* work with Polish people!"

"Brother Kapitaniuk! Over here!" A short, heavyset man with thick glasses called my name as I stepped down from the train. His bushy, dark hair was streaked with gray and his angular face was unsmiling as I approached him.

I smiled as I shook his pudgy hand. "Brother Husaruk! It's good to see you again!"

He eyed me coolly. "Didn't you get my letter?"

"Letter?" I stared at him. "What letter?"

Pastor Husaruk smiled wanly. "I wrote you not to come because the president of the Evangelical Union of Canada is speaking to us on Sunday morning."

I hoped I didn't look too disappointed. "I'm sorry, but I never got your letter." I had been in Canada and the States for nearly a year now, and was on my way back to the D.P. camps in Europe. Before leaving America, I had wanted to visit the Slavic church in Montreal where Brother Husaruk was pastor, so I had written to him from Chicago: "Brother, could you arrange a meeting for me on Sunday? I'm passing through Montreal on my way to Europe and would like to minister there." I had posted the letter and waited for a reply. By Thursday I had heard nothing, and I needed to be on my way. So I had caught a train from Chicago to Montreal. The pastor's reply must have arrived in Chicago after I left.

Pastor Husaruk frowned and was silent a moment. "Well," he said, "we can give you five minutes on Sunday morning. But no more."

"Great!" I breathed a silent prayer of thanks. "Five minutes on Sunday morning." My mind raced as I tried to think what I could condense to five minutes. Perhaps something from John 11. I had always liked that chapter. . . .

Sophie picked up the phone to stop its merciless ringing. "Why, hello, Véronique! It's good to hear from you." Sophie was most grateful that her sister was living in Canada during the time of her visit. The two chatted for a few moments in French.

"Sophie," Véronique began carefully, since she knew that she was walking on very thin ice now, "Sophie, would you come to the meeting with me tomorrow?'' She knew of the hard times Sophie had gone through in that church, of the deacon who had falsely accused her.

Sophie was silent for a moment. "No, Véronique,'' she replied softly.

"Oh, Sophie! Why?'' Véronique's voice was not demanding, only concerned.

Sophie paused. "I don't feel at home in that church.'' How could she explain to her sister how she felt when she walked into church and people looked at her disapprovingly. Why, these people were supposed to be her friends, and they had condemned her on the basis of petty gossip. It was easier to simply not go to church for a while.

"I wish you'd come; we have a missionary here. I heard him once in Toronto. He's wonderful!''

"Oh, Véronique, I don't think so.''

"Sophie, I know you don't want to go to that church, but you'd enjoy hearing this missionary. And the president of the Canadian Evangelical Union is also speaking, so hardly anyone from the church will be participating.''

"I don't know. . . .''

"Please, Sophie. I don't want to sit by myself.''

Sophie was beginning to soften, but still she held out. "Véronique, I really don't want to.''

"Please? For me?''

Well, perhaps just this once, Sophie thought. "Oh, all right. But only for you.''

The next day, Sophie kept her head lowered as she entered the church and prayed that no one would notice her. Her stomach was a tight little ball, and she was angry—angry at all these people who didn't understand her, and angry that her sister had persuaded her to come. She raised her head long enough to scan the narthex; there was Véronique, standing by the far doorway as she had said she would. Sophie sighed. Well, she was committed now. If Véronique had not been standing there, she would have turned and bolted out the door.

Véronique smiled and squeezed Sophie's arm as she came and stood next to her. "Thanks for coming, Sophie."

Sophie smiled faintly and lowered her head again. "Could we go in and sit down? I don't want to stand here."

Arm in arm, the two sisters walked into the sanctuary and entered a pew near the back. They slid toward the middle and sat down. Sophie kept her head bowed, the feelings churning within her. She hoped she didn't look as uncomfortable as she felt. Why had she let Véronique talk her into coming? What could these people teach her but more lies, more distrust, more misery? Well, she wouldn't be here much longer; she was scheduled to leave for France in about two weeks. For her sister's sake she could sit through a service, but for no other reason. She would just tune out everything that was said. Sophie set her jaw, pursed her lips, and stared at her lap. France—she'd think about her beloved France.

After the first hymn, Véronique glanced over at her sister and wondered where her thoughts had taken her. *Perhaps,* thought Véronique, *I don't know the half of what has happened here.* She gave Sophie a gentle nudge. "Sophie, the missionary—he's about to speak. You listen, all right?"

Sophie nodded glumly. "Yeah, sure." She continued to stare at her hands. She really didn't want to listen to what anybody had to say—missionary or not.

But she couldn't help hearing the deep, resonant voice that followed. "In the opening verse of the eleventh chapter of John," the voice began, "we read that Lazarus of Bethany, brother of Mary and Martha, was sick. So Mary and Martha sent a servant to find Jesus." The voice paused. "What did the servant say when he found Him?"

After a brief silence, a very familiar voice, which sounded far away, answered, "Lord, if You had been here, our brother would not have died!" Sophie winced at the very sound of that voice; it was the deacon who had falsely accused her.

But the missionary replied, "No." And at that, Sophie lifted her head. She spotted the deacon sitting in the choir loft behind the pulpit. His face was flushed and he looked very embarrassed. *Good for that missionary!* thought Sophie. And she turned her eyes toward the man in the pulpit.

He was tall and lanky with very broad shoulders. Sophie was struck by his rugged good looks. *He must be about twenty-five,* she thought. Despite her intentions, she found herself listening to what he had to say.

"The right answer is this," continued the missionary. "The servant came to Jesus and said, 'Lord, behold, he whom You love is sick.' Now, why didn't the servant tell Jesus to come and heal Lazarus? Why didn't he tell Jesus to hurry because Lazarus was dying? This would have been the natural thing, the thing you or I would have done. If someone in our family were dying we would go to a doctor and say two words: 'Come!' and 'Quickly!' But the servant didn't say 'come' and he didn't say 'quickly.' Why not? I think the key is found in the first word that the servant used to address Jesus: 'Lord.'

"If Jesus is Lord, then this servant was a slave. And a slave never gives orders to his master; he would never tell his master to 'do this' or 'do that.' A young soldier never gives orders to his general. And Christians should not be giving orders to their Lord. All we can do is open our hearts before Him and make our needs known. And this is what that servant did. He said, 'Lord . . . he whom You love is sick.'

"Another thing that strikes me from this passage," the missionary continued, "is the way the servant said, 'Lord . . . he whom You love. . . .' The servant didn't say, 'Lord, Lazarus who loves you is sick.' Often we do that. We say, 'Lord, this person who loves you, this person who's been so faithful, this person who's been sacrificing, he's sick.' But the servant was so convinced of the love that the Lord had for Lazarus that he said, '. . . he whom You love. . . .'

"We can read this passage with what Paul said to the Philippians in chapter four, verses six and seven: 'Be anxious for nothing, but in everything by prayer and supplication with thanksgiving let your requests be made known to God. And the peace of God, which surpasses all comprehension, shall guard your hearts and your minds in Christ Jesus.' The servant returned to Mary and Martha with the peace of God in his heart, because he did his part in making their requests known to Jesus Christ, and leaving the final decision with Him who is the Master.'' With this, the missionary turned and sat down.

"Thank you, Brother Kapitaniuk.'' Pastor Husaruk rose and addressed the congregation. . . .

The service over, Sophie and Véronique made their way quickly out of the church and began scanning the mass of people. Sophie's heart had been touched by what the missionary had said and she wanted a word with him. Suddenly Véronique grabbed her arm. "There he is, Sophie, over there.'' She pointed to a small group of people standing under a maple tree. The missionary towered over everyone.

As Sophie approached, he appeared to be in a deep discussion with a middle-aged man. The two of them held their open Bibles and pointed out passages to each other, nodding and speaking animatedly. Soon the missionary clapped the old man on the back and they shook hands and exchanged good-byes. Then he turned to Sophie and smiled. His blue eyes were dancing.

She extended her hand and returned his smile. "Hello, Brother Kapitaniuk,'' she began, "my name is Sophie Bobel.''

His large hand enclosed hers in a firm grip. "Bill Kapitaniuk,'' he replied. His voice was resonant even in the open air.

"I enjoyed your talk,'' Sophie added. "If you ever come to France, I'd like you to come and speak to the young people in our church in Calvados. Here's my address.''

Bill Kapitaniuk pulled a small notebook from the pocket of his suitcoat, and Sophie was amazed at the number of names and addresses that were written in it. But he took hers down dutifully, then smiled and said, "Thanks!'' She walked past him a few steps to where her sister was waiting; several more people wanted to speak with him.

Later that day, Sophie's teacup clattered as she set it on the

thin china saucer. It had been a lovely meal and she sat back
and sighed contentedly. She was feeling better than she had for
days. Much though she had protested, she was glad her sister
had dragged her off to church. The spiritual uplift had been
just what she needed. And it felt good to laugh again with
Véronique and Véronique's roommate, Sarah.

As the three sat around the table, Sarah turned to Sophie.
Sarah was a Christian Jewess, a vivacious girl. Her face had
become suddenly serious and, as Sophie later reflected, confident. "Sophie" she said, "you know that man who preached
today? He's going to be your husband one day."

Sophie stared blankly back at Sarah. She didn't laugh. She
didn't argue. She didn't ask Sarah to explain what she meant.
She just sat there staring, as if she were dumb. She found that
she couldn't react because, well, she felt absolutely nothing for
this man. She had barely met him! Why would Sarah say
something like that? How could she be so sure? Sophie looked
down at the table and said nothing. There was nothing she
could say.

I sat lost in thought as I chewed my dark bread and cheese in
silence. A few months had passed since the service in Montreal, and
fall was not far away. I was back in Europe, working in the D.P.
camps among the people I loved—encouraging, sharing, challenging. Again I was struck by the openness, the thirst for the gospel, the
way the refugees eagerly devoured my messages and waited
hungrily for more. *What must it be like in their homelands?* I often
wondered. And I began to dream of visiting Eastern Europe some
day to see for myself.

An additional blessing was my improved ability to preach, to
share, to discuss in Polish. My three years of working in the
Polish-French church in Belgium had not only given me valuable
experience, they had also given me two new languages. It was
heartwarming to see the light dawn on Polish faces as I presented
the gospel to them in their own language. These Polish people
continued to intrigue me, and the love I had had for my flock in Liège
began to resurface as love for these dear folk.

I finished my lunch and, while my thoughts rambled, began to finger the envelope I had stuffed into my shirt pocket earlier. I pulled it out, removed the enclosed letter and reread it.

I folded the letter and gazed out on my peaceful surroundings. A few cows were grazing nearby, wandering over the lush hillside. A calf in a far corner of the field, having lost sight of its mother, bawled plaintively. A warm breeze rustled the leaves of the huge ash tree that rose majestically behind me. My thoughts drifted far away, to Montreal, Canada, and a maple tree garbed in fresh spring leaves, under which I had talked to a somewhat flushed and nervous young Slavic girl.

I could not recall her features exactly, but her dark eyes still returned to look at me with a mixture of wonder and unease. Sophie Bobel. We had been corresponding since that chance meeting. Could I really call it "chance"? The more we corresponded, the closer I was drawn to her. Like me, she had had difficulties in her walk with the Lord. Like me, she had been misunderstood and had been falsely accused. Her problems had made her despondent, and the despair came through in her letters.

And, yet, it was not a total despair. She seemed to be groping for something to prove that all those people had been wrong and that the Lord was victorious. I sensed in her a faith that held on despite obstacles, a spirit that pressed on when faced with difficulties. It was this spirit that drew me to her, because she had not had life easy, but she also had not given up hope. More and more I found myself thinking of her and looking forward to her notes. Day by day I began to feel that ours was no casual correspondence, but the Lord had arranged our meeting in Montreal for something more serious. In my heart I had begun to believe that our relationship would result in a marriage one day.

As I sat beneath that ash tree, I remembered Sophie's gentle plea to come and speak to the young people in her church. Perhaps the time had come to pay a visit to Monsieur and Madame Bobel and their daughter. . . .

"Mais, oui ! Of course I'd like to go to Bible school!"
Sophie sat on the sofa in her parents' living room and looked

at the pastor who had come from Paris. He knew she had not completed her studies in Canada and was giving her a chance to finish. "But," she added, "my parents aren't rich. I can't afford Bible school in Paris."

"Oh, no, no—you won't need to pay for any of it. We'll pay for all the expenses."

For all the expenses? Such generosity was almost too good to be true! But Sophie responded, "Give me some time to talk it over with my parents first." Actually, Bible school in Paris would be a great idea, because then Sophie would not be too far from her folks. She had missed her mother terribly the four years she had spent in Canada. Her mother had a way of speaking to her heart, and if Sophie studied in Paris, she could travel home periodically without much difficulty. After her struggles in Canada, Sophie needed her mother's soothing presence. Perhaps this was God's way of helping her get over the struggles of the past four years. . . .

It was mid-afternoon by the time I found the two-storied yellow stucco building in the small village of Giberville, Calvados. It was typical of the large, European apartment-type buildings of that time. I compared the number on the building with my address book: 5, rue du Bois. Yes, this was indeed Sophie's house. I approached the door and knocked. After what seemed like several minutes, a short, stout woman with graying hair emerged and eyed me cautiously. *"Oui?"*

I smiled, "Madame Bobel?"

Her curt *"Oui"* was more of a grunt than anything else.

I extended my hand. "Bill Kapitaniuk."

My name made no impression on her; she ignored my hand and continued to look me up and down. Finally her eyes rested on my face and she glared at me.

"I'm your daughter Sophie's friend."

At that her eyebrows rose appreciably. *"Ah, oui? Attends ici!"* With that, her buxom frame disappeared inside the house and a moment later she returned with Sophie peering surprisedly over her shoulder "Bill! How nice to see you again!" She paused long enough for me to take in the dark, gentle eyes, the distinctly Slavic face. She had a kerchief round her head and wore a faded apron. "I didn't know you were in Calvados."

Later that day, I sat in the living room with Monsieur Bobel discussing what I would say in the worship service the next day. We had eaten dinner together, and Madame Bobel, Sophie, and her sister Janine were busy doing the dishes. Once I had been introduced and the Bobels realized that I was the one who had been writing to their daughter, I was openly accepted as a welcome guest and treated warmly. Sophie had been taken aback that I had arrived without writing to let her know precisely when I was coming, but she was not angry. As her father and I were in the midst of our discussion, Sophie appeared in the doorway. "Bill? You mentioned that your suit jacket needs pressing for tomorrow. I'd be happy to do it for you."

"That would be good! I'll go get it out of my suitcase." I rose and followed her out of the room. I strode into the guest room, pulled the crumpled jacket from my things, and handed it to Sophie with a sheepish grin. "Can you do anything with this?"

Sophie smiled and took the jacket without saying a word. I walked with her to the back of the house where baskets overflowed with clean clothes; shirts, dresses and other items hung from pegs on the wall. She set up the ironing board and arranged my jacket on it as she waited for the iron to heat. As she began to iron, I shoved my hands into my pockets and asked, "So, tell me more about what the pastor from Paris had to say this morning."

She looked up at me and started to explain: "Well, there's a Bible school in Paris, a good one, and this pastor told me that he would pay all my expenses if I went. I think it's a good idea. It's not too far from home, and. . . ."

"Sophie," I interrupted her softly, walking over to where she was ironing. I had noticed that she was putting sharp creases in my lapels. I hated to say anything to her, especially since I was sure home economics had been part of her school curriculum, but I was thinking of the future now. If she was to be my wife some day, she might as well learn now how I liked my suit jackets pressed! I continued, "You know, the lapels need to be round and not sharp."

For a second, Sophie looked as though she had been slapped. But she said nothing and adjusted the lapels. A few minutes later we were back in the living room, sitting with her parents and talking about the Lord. Mme. Bobel had a lot of questions, and we had a great time discussing Bible texts. It was very late that night when we climbed the stairs to our rooms.

The midmorning sun filtered through the kitchen window and formed a rectangle of gold on the kitchen table where Sophie was chopping vegetables. Her mother and Janine had gone to town to buy meat and a few other items for their midday meal, and Bill and her father were in the living room talking. At last she had a few moments to herself to think through the events of the past few days.

Almost a week had passed since Bill had arrived. Those few days had been some of the happiest that Sophie could remember. She and Janine and Bill had spent many hours talking and laughing together. And in the evenings Sophie and her parents and Bill would stay up for hours discussing the Bible. Her parents were growing quite fond of Bill, she could tell, and the church had enjoyed having him speak.

It was a pity that he would be leaving soon. Sophie found that she was happy just being in his company. She felt a certain calm within as he spoke, almost like a balm to her soul. And he had such marvelous insights into the Bible! He could talk about his faith much the way her mother could. Perhaps that was why she enjoyed being with him so much. He had a knack of touching her heart with what he said, and often he would speak to her deepest needs without his even knowing it. The bad memories from her four years in Canada were slowly fading. . . .

The air had a characteristic nip to it as I helped Sophie pull in the laundry. It was beginning to really feel like fall. Soon, very soon, I would have to return to the D.P. camps in Germany.

The past few days had been pure delight. Sophie's folks were wonderful people. They loved the Lord wholeheartedly, and I found myself looking forward to our evenings of discussion together. And it had been good to use my Polish some more! I was glad to see that my year in America had not completely spoiled what little I knew of the language.

And then, of course, there was Sophie. The more time I spent with her, the surer I was that she would be my wife one day. She had a beautiful walk with the Lord and a hunger to know and love Him more that was a joy to see. It was, in fact, one of the things that drew

me to her. The Lord seemed to have arranged everything! "Lord," I had prayed last night, "the way everything has come together, I accept that as from You."

I had no idea when I would be in France again after tomorrow. A bit hesitantly, I turned to Sophie. "You know that tomorrow I'm leaving for Belgium and then for Germany?" She nodded without looking at me. "There's something I'd like to talk about with you." She raised her head to meet my gaze. Could she possibly know what I wanted to ask her? "Sophie, will you marry me and work for the Lord alongside me?"

The shirt that Sophie had been folding fell to the ground as she looked at me in utter astonishment. Before she had time to collect herself, I continued. "Think hard about your answer before you say anything. Because I'm a missionary, I won't be able to stay with you all the time. I have to travel a lot. It won't be an easy life."

We stood and stared at each other in silence. I could imagine Sophie's shock. During the week of my visit, we had never talked about a serious relationship developing between us. We were always with or near someone else. This was the first real chance I had had to talk with her alone.

But there was more than uncertainty in her eyes. Was it fear? Finally she said softly, "I don't know. Let me pray about it tonight."

Well, what had I expected? I certainly had to respect her honesty and her desire to seek the Lord's guidance. I would just have to wait until tomorrow. . . .

Sophie heard the clock in the downstairs hallway chime two as she lay awake thinking. Janine, as usual, had been asleep when, after the now-routine evening of Bible discussion, Sophie had opened the door to the room they shared. But hours had passed since then, and Janine's snores only served to accent Sophie's sleeplessness. She wondered if Bill had fallen asleep yet or if sleep eluded him also.

The clock's ticking downstairs seemed so loud, and with each stroke her stomach churned a bit more. She had to keep telling herself to stay calm. How could she tell Bill that she was scared to death of marriage—not just to him, but to anybody? She hoped he had not seen the fear that had gripped her when he broached the subject. After an experience that she had had in Canada, Sophie found it difficult to trust men— all men. The thought of marriage was too much: the ultimate form of trust. Now her fear would be discovered, and she had nowhere to hide. Why did that clock keep ticking so? She couldn't think with its ticking.

Besides, she hardly knew Bill! She liked him a lot, but she could not say that she loved him. Yet, she had a peculiar feeling that she should not refuse his proposal. Asking him to wait was all she could think to do at that moment. Now she felt terribly confused. How could she possibly have an answer for him tomorrow?

"Dear, dear Lord," Sophie whispered, "You know that Bill is a good man, a godly man. Please, if You want me to marry him, give me something special for him. And soon, Lord—he's leaving tomorrow!"

I thought I would burst with joy as I looked down at my new fiancée. She seemed somehow changed since yesterday. Or had I changed? No, her face possessed a serenity that was not there before. And her eyes—her eyes were peaceful. No uncertainty, no fear today. Her joy bubbled over and added to mine. Yes, I could see that the Lord had worked a miracle overnight. She had told me of her prayer. *Oh,* I thought, *the Lord is good!*

Sophie grabbed my arm and pulled me toward the kitchen. "You go and ask my mother now!" Even her eyes were laughing. So I left her in the sitting room and went into the kitchen, where her mother was sitting at the table peeling potatoes. "Good morning, Madame Bobel," I began.

She looked up from her work and smiled warmly. "Oh, good morning, Bill."

"Madame Bobel, I'd like to take Sophie to work with me in Austria."

Her smile quickly faded, and she shook her head. "Oh, no. Never!" She glared at me as though I had just crossed the border into an area where I had no right to be. I could see the wheels turning. "Does he know what he's asking?'' she seemed to be thinking. "How dare he? Take my daughter to Austria! They're not married!'' I could barely suppress the chuckle under my breath.

Sophie poked her head through the doorway. "Bill,'' she pretended to scold, her eyes twinkling, "that's not the way to ask for my hand!'' She giggled and my own chuckles became louder.

But Sophie's mother was not laughing. Even with Sophie's comment, she did not understand what was going on. I decided that perhaps this was not the best time to tease her. I stopped chuckling, looked at her, and said, "What if I were to marry Sophie first? Then could I take her with me?''

"Oh,'' she blurted, "*that* way! That changes everything! In that case I have no objection!'' The scowl disappeared and we all began to laugh. Mme. Bobel wiped her hands on her apron, rose from her chair, and gathered Sophie and me into her arms. We were all happily discussing our future plans when we heard Sophie's father come in from weeding the garden.

Sophie froze. "Oh, Mother,'' she said, "you tell Papa! We don't feel brave enough to tell him! Bill didn't ask you properly; he can't make that mistake with Papa. Please!'' She looked imploringly at her mother.

M. Bobel marched through the kitchen door in his work clothes and galoshes. He stopped long enough to remove the galoshes, then nodded to us and headed toward his bedroom to change. Sophie's mother followed him into the bedroom and closed the door. I could hear her voice, but could not make out what she was saying.

Moments later, Sophie's father emerged from the bedroom and strode into the kitchen. His face was stern as he studied me in silence, and I began to wonder just what his wife had said to him. Then his mouth broke into a grin as he asked, "So, when are you two getting married?'' The tension broken, we all laughed. He came over and pumped my arm. "I'm very happy and proud to have you as a son-in-law,'' he added. Later I discovered that, of the five Bobel children, only Sophie had chosen to marry a Christian.

The weather had turned cooler as my train neared Calvados. Several weeks had passed since Sophie had agreed to marry me.

After a quick visit to my old church in Belgium, I had spent the time with refugees at the D.P. camps in Austria and Germany. Once again, I was deeply touched by the hunger and the responsiveness of these dear people.

In my pocket I carried a surprise for Sophie. While visiting Munich one day, I noticed an old basement shop with a display of unusual jewelry. As I walked in and looked over the different rings, my eyes fell upon just the kind I had envisioned, with one diamond in the center and a little stone on each side. After rummaging through several other shops, I had not found a ring I liked as well, so I returned to buy it. Since I had not even measured Sophie's finger, I had no idea if it would fit, but I bought it anyway.

My reception at Sophie's home was much warmer than on my previous visit, and soon we were all talking and laughing around the dinner table. After the dishes were all done and put away, I led Sophie into the living room.

We sat down on the sofa and, after a moment, I said to Sophie, "Close your eyes and let me see your hand." Sophie obediently shut her eyes and put her left hand behind her back. With heart pounding, I took the ring out of my pocket and slipped it onto her finger. I stared in amazement; the ring fit perfectly!

On December 29, 1956, six months after our "chance" meeting in Montreal, Sophie and I were married in Caen, France. The ceremony was a simple one in a small Reformed church, and fifteen people attended the turkey dinner that followed, prepared by Sophie's mother and aunt. Sophie and I were very poor at that time—so poor, in fact, that my mother-in-law had to buy my wedding shoes! But we were both convinced that the Lord had drawn us together, and we anxiously awaited what now lay ahead.

The pieces were slowly fitting together: my Ukrainian background, Bible school, the decision to become a missionary to my own Slavic people, the chance to evangelize, three years as a pastor of a Polish-French church, a growing love and concern for the Polish people especially, a French-Polish wife. The Lord had truly prepared the backdrop for what was to become a unique work.

5

Sizzling Sausages

A light snow was falling as I gathered my belongings and clambered aboard the eastbound train in Vienna. A blast of warmth hit my bare face and then enveloped me as I opened the door and made my way down the narrow corridor toward the second-class compartments. Finding one vacant, I eased my small suitcase and bulging food sacks onto a seat and collapsed on the one opposite. At long last I was headed for Poland!

About a year had elapsed since my wedding. Sophie and I had spent much of that time working among refugees in the D.P. camps of West Germany. Money was tight, but we managed pretty well, especially since we were able to share an apartment with another missionary couple. But when we discovered that Sophie was pregnant, we decided to return to Calvados. There, on October 17, 1957, our son Daniel was born.

While in Calvados, helping in the church in any way I could, I heard that there had been a change in the Polish government, and that there was now freedom to enter and travel in that country. My heart leaped at the news! Could this be the chance I had been waiting for? As I prayed about it, I felt in my heart that God was asking me to go there. So I left Sophie and the baby and headed for Eastern Europe, with an aunt's address my only internal link.

I breathed on the frosty train window and wiped it with my sleeve. Dusk was falling, and the dimmed light cast long shadows from the city buildings onto the streets. Several bundled forms shuffled past, clutching parcels tightly against themselves in an effort to ward off the biting wind. The train, though, was very well heated. I removed my winter coat, wool hat, scarf, and gloves. I was still alone in my compartment, and it was so quiet that I wondered if I was the only passenger on that train car.

After picking up my Polish and Czech visas and my train ticket, I had bought a little food for the trip: fruit, dark bread, and Austrian sausages. I pulled some of the sausages out of a sack and placed them on the steam pipes in my compartment. In minutes they were sizzling hot. I feasted on dark bread and hot sausages as I waited for the train to leave.

Soon after, the train pulled out of the station. I was really on my way to Poland! I settled back in my seat and tried to imagine what it would be like. I must have dozed off, because the next thing I knew, a man's deep voice was announcing, in German, that we were approaching the Czech border. I glanced at my watch: 8:00 P.M. Heart pounding, I cleared a space on the window to have a look.

It was completely dark. As my eyes adjusted, I could make out the wooden posts of a guard tower. Several spotlights at the top of the tower cast their wide beams downward onto our train. Large feathery snowflakes drifted down through the light beams and joined the already-thick blanket of snow, muffling the sound of our entry into Czechoslovakia. Slowly the train wheels squealed to a halt.

Then I saw them: soldiers everywhere. They seemed to have jumped out of nowhere with their guns, taking positions at the front of the train, at the back, along the sides. Here and there, snarling German shepherds padded obediently alongside their masters, stopping at intervals as the soldiers positioned themselves.

I gasped. I had never seen anything like this. Why were all these soldiers with guns watching our train? Beyond them I could see the dark outlines of the border-complex buildings, and—as the spotlights continued to cast their searching rays— I could detect a rough network of barbed wire framing the scene. The soft, silently falling snow added a dimension of eerie stillness. For a long time I sat staring out the window, trying to sort some meaning from the chilling scene before me.

My contemplation was shattered as a steely-faced customs official burst into my compartment and brusquely asked to see my passport. With silent scrutiny he compared my passport and visa photos with my face. Then, with an apparently satisfied grunt, he handed the passport back to me and was gone.

Once again I took up my silent vigil at the window. The soldiers remained in their positions, their breaths forming small clouds around their faces each time they exhaled. Suddenly the train jerked and we began inching forward. I looked at my watch; we had been at the border for over an hour.

I had saved a few Austrian sausages, hoping to sizzle them on the steam pipes as before, but the further we traveled into Czechoslovakia, the colder the train became. Soon I donned my woolen coat again and, not long after, my hat and gloves. By early morning there was no heat in the train. Shivering, huddled in a thin blanket in a corner of the seat, I dozed sporadically.

"Herbata goraca! Herbata goraca!"

Sleepily, I opened one eye and listened. Silence. Perhaps I was only dreaming.

"Herbata goraca! Herbata goraca!"

The sound of the familiar Polish kept tugging at my drowsy

consciousness until I sat up with a jolt. This was no dream. I
was really hearing Polish! Had we reached the Polish border?

"*Herbata goraca! Herbata goraca! Herbata goraca!*"

I reached up in the dark to flip on the light switch: 4:00 A.M.
I rubbed my eyes and unwound myself from the blanket.

"*Herbata goraca! Herbata goraca!*"

Hot tea! Someone was selling hot tea! I stumbled to my feet
and slid open the door to my compartment. Squinting, I tried
to determine the source of that voice. Shuffling down the
corridor toward me was a hunched little woman carrying a tray
laden with steaming cups. Wisps of gray hair peeked out from
her kerchief, and she was wrapped in a black woolen shawl.
Her huge rubber boots looked out of place on her tiny body.
She smiled up at me. "*Herbata goraca?*"

What a thrill, despite the cold, that I could understand what
she was saying! I refused her offer, saying that I had no money
to pay for it.

She looked puzzled. "But it's free," she responded in Polish.

Free tea! What a contrast to our reception in Czechoslovakia. As I sipped gratefully, my heart was warmed to think that
here, on a cold train, we were offered free hot tea. And as I
think back now, what a fitting introduction to the warmth,
the hospitality, the openness, of my beloved friends, the Polish
people.

"Excuse me." I reached out a hand and touched the coat of
a middle-aged man passing by me on the sidewalk. "Can you
tell me if there are any Baptist churches in the area?" As he
stared, I continued, "Or, do you know any Baptists?" (In that
setting, "Baptist" was synonymous with "evangelical.")

But my eyes met the same blank look to which I had
quickly become accustomed during my first week in Poland.
"No. I don't know any." He dug his hands deeper into his
pockets and walked on, his feet crunching the packed snow.

The only Polish address I had was my aunt's, in the city of
Szczecin, so when I arrived in Warsaw I had to stay at a hotel.
I decided to remain there for a while to see if I could find any

evangelical Christians. Every day I ventured out and posed my two questions to as many people as I could on the cold winter streets. But the answer was always the same. No one knew of any Baptists or of any Baptist churches. After a week of this, I decided the sensible thing to do was take another train and travel the 375 miles to Szczecin and visit my aunt.

My mother's oldest sister greeted me warmly. We had never met, and she was overjoyed to see her nephew from Canada. I, in turn, enjoyed meeting her and some other relatives, but we had no close fellowship because she did not share my evangelical Christian faith. And, to my dismay, she also knew of no evangelical churches in the area.

While staying with her, I ventured into the center of town and began inquiring of the people there whether they knew of any Baptists or Baptist churches. I had a Polish Bible with me and also some tracts, and in every home I entered I gave out tracts and tried to read some Scripture. Everyone looked at me as though I were from another planet. I was very naive and did not realize at the time that it was against the country's laws to distribute literature—in fact, it was very dangerous. And, on top of that, most people I talked with were Roman Catholic and would ask, "What kind of Bible do you have? Does it have the Pope's imprimatur?" Since, of course, I had a Protestant Bible, often they would push me out saying, "That's not our Bible; that's no good!"

Finally, someone pointed down a street and said, "In that house over there is someone like you." With great anticipation I headed for the little house. I knocked and opened the door a crack to see a lady sitting by a table reading a Bible. At last! I thought I had finally found an evangelical Christian. We began to talk, and I asked the woman about her faith.

"I'm a Jehovah's Witness," she replied.

My heart sank.

But, surprisingly, this woman had the best news I'd heard since entering Poland! "There are some Baptists in the next town of Stargard."

I stamped my feet, trying to shake off the cold. More snow had fallen during the night, but the morning air was clear and crisp. The early train ride to Stargard had been very short, and now I found myself on the cold streets once again, asking everyone I saw, "Do you know of a Baptist church?" And again they all shook their heads. After hours of aimless wandering, I came to a hill and noticed a Catholic church at the top. I went in and started asking people my usual question. One of the priests said, "Yes, there's a Baptist church down the road from here."

Once again I set off, walking in the direction that he had indicated. I had to pick my way through the rubble, because Stargard had been devastated during World War II. After I had stumbled along for several minutes, I came upon a little stream and saw a man crossing the bridge. "Sir," I called out in Polish, "do you know where the Baptist church is?"

My voice startled him and he staggered a moment, but steadied himself on the bridge railing. Then he thrust out his hand and pointed in the direction of the Catholic church from which I had just come.

I shook my head. "No, that's the Catholic church. Where is the *Baptist* church?"

I was near him now and could see that he was drunk. He stumbled off the bridge and down the path towards me. He grabbed my arm to keep from falling. "Oh, it's not far from here." He gave me directions and then staggered off.

I set off across the bridge as he had indicated and had not walked very far before I saw a red brick building: the Baptist church! As I stood wondering how I was going to find the pastor, I spotted the mailman making his rounds. I pointed to the church and asked him, "Sir, do you know where the pastor lives?"

He nodded. "Come with me." And the two of us continued down the street, chatting in Polish. After we walked awhile, he jutted his chin toward a small, plain house (his hands were full of mail). "This is where the pastor lives."

I thanked him, walked up to the door and knocked. A middle-aged lady appeared, and I smiled and said, "*Chwala Panu!*" Praise the Lord!

Her face broke into a wide grin. "*Chwala Panu!* Who are you? Where are you from?"

Had I at last found some evangelical Christians? "I'm a missionary from Canada—"

She rushed at me, hugged me, kissed me. "From Canada! This is the first time anyone from so far away has come here!"

She was the pastor's wife, and shortly afterward I met the pastor and their three sons. I spent several days with them and had many opportunities to participate and preach in their church (the Baptist church of Szczecin-Stargard). I also obtained the address of the Central Committee of the Evangelical Union in Warsaw. Delighted that at last I had found some like-minded believers, I made my way back to Warsaw.

Nearly a dozen pairs of cold, suspicious eyes studied me in unison from head to foot. It was a cold Saturday afternoon at the office of the Central Committee of the Evangelical Union in Warsaw. When I began to speak in my mixture of Ukrainian and Polish with my obvious Ukrainian accent, they became even more guarded. "I'm a missionary from Canada," I began.

The committee members were seated around an enormous oval table, serious and somber-faced. Although they asked few questions, the entire time I was conscious of their eyes upon me—calculating, cautious eyes, willing to take no risks. At that time, few foreigners were coming into Poland, and these men were not ready to unreservedly accept as an authentic Christian every person who arrived on their doorstep.

At last they invited me to be seated, and I listened to the various agenda items being discussed. Most of their business did not interest me, but one question that the president addressed to the secretary caught my attention: "Would you send a telegram to Bialystok, saying that we have no one to go to the church on Sunday morning?"

Murmurs and nods around the table indicated assent, and I watched the secretary jot the request in his notebook. Discussion for the day seemed to be winding down, and I ventured to address the president. "Excuse me." My voice sounded small and insignificant in the midst of the older, solemn faces surrounding me. I could feel their skeptical eyes on me once again, but I plunged ahead. "I'm willing to go to that church. If you have nobody, I'd be very happy to go and minister there."

The president eyed me up and down once more. His eyes softened a little as he spoke to me. "You are willing?"

"Yes, sir." I answered without hesitation, lest by thinking things over I might be tempted to change my mind.

The president nodded, gazing thoughtfully at the table. When he spoke again, his tone was decisive. "Very well. You can go. We'll send a brother with you." His eyes searched the faces around the table and came to rest on a heavyset colleague with gray, bushy hair. "Brother Stawinski, you will accompany Brother Kapitaniuk to Bialystok."

The small waiting room at Warsaw's Prague Station wasn't very crowded. I glanced anxiously at the clock: 4:50 P.M. The train for Bialystok was scheduled to leave at 5:00 P.M.

Stawinski and I had arranged to meet at 4:30, but there was no sign of him. Had I misunderstood our meeting place? I picked up my small suitcase and approached some people standing near the doorway. "Is this the station where the train leaves for Bialystok?"

"Oh, no," one woman responded, "you have to go around the block. That's the main station. This is just a small waiting room."

With that, I was out the door and fairly flew around the corner. Then I saw the tracks and the station, sprawled before me like a huge maze of wood and steel—and people. Hundreds of them swarmed over the tracks, on the platform, in front of the ticket booths, and at the doorways to a waiting train—the train to Bialystok. I elbowed my way through the crowd, arriving breathlessly at the ticket counter. "Please," I gasped, "give me a ticket for Bialystok! The train is leaving in a minute!"

Ticket in hand, I shoved back through the mass of people. But just as I reached the platform the train was pulling away. Now what? Suddenly I remembered that I had the phone number for the Evangelical Union Central Committee office. I found a phone booth and tried to call, but the phone was out of order. Frantically I banged it, my mind reeling. I'd better try another phone. Then, as I turned around, I saw Stawinski.

Relief shone on both our faces. "Praise the Lord!" I grinned, clapping him on the back. "Let's go get something hot to drink." Armed with steaming mugs of cocoa to ward off the effects of the cold, we walked across the tracks to find a posted train schedule. The next train to Bialystok would leave at 7:20 P.M. As we walked on a bit further, we saw a train marked, "Warsaw–Bialystok." It was an old train, unlike most of the passenger trains I was used to, but that did not bother me.

Stawinski smiled. "Good! Now that we know where our train is, let's go find a little place to rest." I agreed, and on the next track we spotted a first-class modern train. We both had the same idea: "Let's go in there to get warm and rest." So we climbed aboard and found ourselves an empty compartment. It was quite warm and Stawinski fell asleep as I read a newspaper. About seven o'clock I nudged him. "We'd better go back and get on that train to Bialystok."

We left our cozy surroundings and boarded the train marked, "Warsaw-Bialystok." We waited till 7:20 but nothing happened. I was becoming uneasy. I noticed a train conductor across the aisle and went over to him. "Excuse me, sir. Isn't this train going to Bialystok at seven-twenty?

He frowned. "Well, no. Come here to the window. You can see that train to Bialystok just leaving over there." He pointed to a moving train a couple of tracks away. Then he turned to me. "This train goes to Bialystok, but it's a local milk train. It leaves at nine and picks up all the milk along the way."

I groaned. No wonder this didn't look like a regular passenger train! Now we had missed the second train because we did not have our information correct. I went back to our seat and told Brother Stawinski what had happened. All we could do was wait. At 9:00 P.M., our milk train pulled out. But instead of traveling on a one-hour express, we stopped at every local station and didn't reach Bialystok until midnight.

Now we were faced with a new problem: where to spend the night. It was too late to find lodging, so we used the waiting room at the station. There were some huge tables, and we sat at one with our suitcases wedged between our feet. Then we lay our heads on our arms on the wide wooden tabletop and fell into an exhausted sleep.

"Son, what a joy it is to meet a young man like you, all the way from another world!" A husky man in his early seventies, grinning from ear to ear, grasped my hand and shook it with a vigor that surprised me. His enormous nose would have been the first thing that arrested your attention, had not a pair of dark-rimmed glasses been perched on it. Most of his front teeth must have been gold, for as they reflected the early morning sun I was momentarily blinded. "I'm Brother Zombrowski," he added.

Smiling broadly, I returned his handshake. I was glad that Brother Stawinski and I had gotten up at seven o'clock and taken a taxi to the large wooden house where the Sunday worship service services were be be held. Now we had a little time to catch our breath before the services began. People were arriving, though, and soon the house was full to the rafters. It struck me that the people were dressed very poorly, especially for winter.

At 9:00 A.M. the service began with singing. And what singing! Lusty from-the-heart voices that filled the house and must have been heard in the surrounding village. We sang several hymns and then I was asked to preach. After that, we had an extended time of prayer, and by then it was time for lunch. The people greeted me warmly and seemed genuinely

„NIEBO I ZIEMIA PRZEMI-
NĄ, ALE SŁOWA MOJE
NIE PRZEMINĄ."

Łuk. 21,33

appreciative of my presence with them. I was reminded of the
Slavic people I had met in the D.P. camps. These folk certainly
echoed the same warmth, hospitality, and eagerness to hear
the gospel.

In the afternoon, we came together again for more singing,
a time of discussion, preaching, praying, and a question-and-
answer session. This cycle continued until 11:00 P.M.! By then
I was tired, not being used to the typical East European Slavic
meetings. That day I learned that the Polish style was for
Sunday services to go on for hours and hours.

At eleven that night, Brother Stawinski and I took a taxi
back to the train station and waited for the midnight train to
Warsaw. Well, if we had thought that nothing could surpass
our milk-train experience, we were sadly mistaken. When I
opened the door to the train, I nearly fell over from the
smell. On this train, people were not the only passengers; there
were also pigs, chickens, geese, and ducks. Farmers were
on their way to the Monday-morning market in Warsaw, so
they had everything on that train! And, like the milk train,
this one stopped at every station, picking up more people
and animals at each stop. We did not arrive in Warsaw until
four in the morning! I made my way to the hotel and fell
into bed; I was dead tired and slept until about four that
afternoon.

Shortly after this was New Year's, which meant special
services in the churches. The Evangelical Union must have
been pleased with my participation in Bialystok because I was
invited to speak in both of Warsaw's Evangelical Union
churches.

The first service began at 10:00 P.M. and continued till
midnight. Then some brothers drove me to the second church,
where a service was scheduled from midnight till about seven
o'clock in the morning. This second service was similar in
format to regular Sunday meetings, where my preaching was
punctuated by periods of singing, testimonies, poetry recita-
tions, and praying. But, even with the variety, by 5:00 A.M. I
simply could not go on and asked if they would take me to a

place where I could rest. They found a little room and left me there.

At seven o'clock, one of the churchmen woke me and said, "You need to take a train to Lodź, because there's a ten o'clock New Year's service waiting for you!"

I propped myself up on an elbow and gazed at him sleepily. A service at ten? I couldn't help but chuckle. A few days earlier I had been a brother under suspicion, and now I was being saddled with back-to-back services! I hurriedly got up and took the train to Lodź. After the service, I went right back to Warsaw, because I had been asked to speak at a wedding service at four in the afternoon.

And so it went. After that first service in Bialystok, I was deluged with meetings all over the country. And time after time I was amazed at the terrific hunger for expository preaching. The more contact I had with these materially poor but extremely warm and hospitable people, the more my heart was touched.

"Brother, when will you visit our church in Jamno?" I was in the town of Koszalin, where I had spoken at three Sunday services—morning, afternoon, and early evening. We had ended earlier than most churches I had visited: it was only 6:00 P.M. After the benediction, I found myself surrounded by people from another village who wanted me to speak at their church. Their spokesman was a short, middle-aged man with very bushy eyebrows.

"I'm sorry, but tomorrow I must return to Warsaw." I smiled sadly.

The man was undaunted. "Well, if that's the case, you'll have to come and visit us tonight."

Although it was not late, I was tired from the three services. The thought of more preaching. . . . Besides, it was midwinter, cold, with deep snow in this part of the country. Poor roads made travel hazardous, especially at night. "But I have no means of transportation," I protested, "and it's winter."

"Oh, we'll find you transportation." The man disappeared to find a telephone. After a while, he was back. "I've located a government truck and a chauffeur who's willing to take us to Jamno!" he announced proudly.

We did not have long to wait for the truck, and soon we were bouncing over the country roads, dodging snowdrifts and potholes. Around seven o'clock we arrived in front of a little wooden structure and piled out of the truck. All except the chauffeur, who remained in his seat behind the steering wheel.

As we entered the building, I was surprised to see about a hundred people sitting there. They turned around as we came in. A man got up and walked toward me. "Brother, we've been waiting for you for two hours. We've already sung and prayed. You just go ahead and preach!"

So, with barely a moment to catch my breath, I strode up to the platform and began. "If you have a Bible, turn to the eleventh chapter of John, the first verse. . . ." I spoke for an hour about the first few verses of that chapter, an expanded version of what I had said that time in Montreal, when I first met Sophie. Then I sat down.

Nobody got up. Nobody said anything. Nobody moved. After a time, someone called out, "Brother, we'd like to hear some more!"

The congregation hummed with assent, so I rose to the platform again. I continued from the same chapter, verse by verse. I was touched again by how much Jesus loved Lazarus— by the inner heart of Jesus, revealed as He stood by the grave weeping. I spoke of this and of other truths in this chapter. Just simple Bible exposition. Another hour passed and I sat down again.

Again no one moved. At last a voice broke the silence. "Brother, we want to hear some more."

I got up and looked at my watch. "It's nine o'clock already!"

The same voice came right back: "Oh, we have no watches to watch. You just go ahead and preach. We have lots of time!" The congregation rose and sang a few choruses while stretching their legs. Then they settled back in their seats and looked at me expectantly.

I sighed, not too audibly I hoped, and plunged back into John 11. I spoke mainly about the resurrection-of-Lazarus scene and how Jesus, the all-powerful Son of God, waited for mere mortal men to remove the stone from the entrance to the grave. "And who removed it?" I asked. "Those who laid it there." I paused. "To me, this is a picture of many souls that cannot be saved because they are in spiritual graves, and sometimes their very own friends have laid the stones to those graves. We, as Christians, must remove those stones before Christ can speak to those people. Even after Jesus raised Lazarus, He asked those who were there to come and loose Lazarus because he was all tied up with grave clothes. And here again, it was his friends who had put those grave clothes on him." I continued preaching until about ten o'clock. Then I paused, looking out over the congregation. "That's all for tonight."

Murmured ripples of protest moved over the room. At last, one man spoke: "Brother, can't you stay a little bit longer? We have some questions."

I was utterly exhausted, but I did not know when I would be back to see these people again. "Sure, we can discuss a few questions."

"When is the Lord Jesus Christ coming again?" A voice called out the first of many questions. "What are the signs of the times? Where are we in God's calendar?"

I remained for a half hour, trying to answer their questions. But finally, at 10:30 I said, "I must go now, because the chauffeur is out in the truck waiting for me. I must get back." (The chauffeur, a communist, would not come in to the service, but he had agreed to wait in the truck. Hours had passed and it was freezing cold. I knew it was unfair to make him wait any longer.) At last, the congregation allowed me to leave.

Sitting in the truck, jostling toward Koszalin, I thought about my time in Poland. Every bump reminded me how war had devastated the country, how drab everything looked, how poor most of the people were. Yet, the dearth of material prosperity seemed only to accentuate the true pulse of the people I had met here: their warmth, their hospitality, their eagerness and willingness to hear the gospel and listen for hours and hours, the serious questions they posed wherever I traveled. Once again I had been amazed that here people were willing to wait for two hours to hear solid biblical preaching and then to sit for another three and a half hours. And even then, they wanted me to stay longer! As I reflected on the way they looked at me as I spoke—the gentle urgency of their requests for more expository preaching, the almost-tangible hunger for spiritual things—I knew that I must come back to Poland.

I returned to France a different man. After what I had seen, what I had heard, what I had felt, the people of Poland had become a part of me. As I worked in the church in Calvados, my mind wandered back to that group of country folk who had waited for hours in a cold building just to learn a bit more about the Bible. My thoughts were often busy dreaming of ways to meet the spiritual needs of a people I hardly knew but already dearly loved. And my prayers took on a new focus, with my efforts directed at returning to Poland.

I had seen only a tiny glimpse of what real life in Poland was like—the fear, the suspicion, the invisible hand that guided the thoughts, actions, and dreams of each person living under the communist regime—but that glimpse had increased my curiosity to see just how much could be done for the Lord under these conditions. And I knew I would not be satisfied until I found out.

I felt a strange peace that here was my place, here was the work God had prepared me for. Yet, the peace was tinged with an urgency that drove me to try to discover the best ways to meet those needs I had seen. I knew that I would never again be content to look at Poland from a distance.

6

"On the Twenty-fourth Day . . ."

I tore a weed from our little vegetable patch and flung it onto a steadily growing pile. Living with Sophie's parents in Calvados certainly helped with our expenses, and I had always enjoyed working in the soil. As I knelt in the garden, warmed by the late-summer sun, my mind drifted back to a bumpy dirt road in eastern Poland. . . .

I swerved the car suddenly to avoid a chicken that had picked that moment to cross the road. The village was typical of eastern Poland, with row after row of drab gray houses, hard-packed dirt roads, and an array of small, wandering barnyard animals. Old women in dark skirts and kerchiefs either sat talking in clusters or carried bundles along the roadside. Young children laughed and played in the ditches and small yards. I was not far from the Russian border; one evidence was a beautiful new Orthodox church under construction, looking like the Orthodox churches that dot the landscape in the Soviet Union. The structure was striking with its majestic onion-shaped domes, and I stopped the car and got out to have a closer look.

As I circled the building, I spotted a girl in her late teens seated nearby. I moved closer and discovered that she was sketching the church, doing some lovely work. I stopped by her side and asked, "Do you go to this church?"

She looked up at me, her dark eyes clouded. "No. My father is an atheist. We don't believe in God."

Was it my imagination, or did I detect a note of sadness in her voice? I pulled a Polish New Testament from my coat pocket and held it in front of her. "Have you ever read this book, the Bible?"

Her eyes darted from the book to my face, then back to the book. "No, I've never seen one."

"Would you like to have one?" I asked gently.

"Oh, yes!" she quickly replied. Then she hesitated. "My father says there is no God, but the neighbors say that there is a God. I'm very confused. I don't know what the truth is." Shyly she looked up at me. "Where is the truth?"

I turned to John 14:6 and read, "Jesus said . . . 'I am the way, and the truth, and the life; no one comes to the Father, but through Me.' " The girl was staring at me with rapt attention.

When I stopped reading, she took the New Testament from me and turned it over in her hands. She asked, "What do you want for this? How much? I'll pay you for it!"

"No, no. This is a gift."

She frowned, trying to decide what to do. Suddenly she reached down and picked up the sketch she had been working on. "Here, I'll give you this drawing. In fact"—she picked up two other sketches she had already completed—"you can have all the sketches I have with me."

"Bill? Bill!"

My reverie faded and I became conscious that someone was gently shaking my arm. I looked up into Sophie's face. She was flushed and out of breath. Five-year-old Daniel now had two brothers, Philippe, two, and David, one, and another sibling was on the way. Sophie smiled. "What were you dreaming about? I've been trying to get your attention for the last three minutes!"

I smiled sheepishly as I squinted up at her. "Oh, I was just thinking." In the five years that had passed since my first trip to Poland, I had made several more. Often little vignettes from my travels would replay in my mind, and once again I would be caught up in the drama. I had begun to envision a more tangible and systematic means of assistance than I had yet been able to give. Oh, I enjoyed working in the church in Calvados, but my heart was in Poland, where the dearth of Scripture and the spiritual hunger were so evident.

Sophie seemed determined to bring me back to reality. "The pastor is here and wants to talk to you." She tucked a stray lock of hair into her bun. "He's in the kitchen. Mama is preparing tea."

When I arrived at the house, our pastor was seated at the kitchen table, sipping tea. I greeted him cordially and sat down next to him. Sophie and her mother slipped into the other room, and the pastor and I sat in silence for a few moments. Finally he looked at me and began, "Do you remember the church in Billy-Montigny that I mentioned to you several months ago?"

"Yes." How could I forget? About six months earlier, as I was preparing for a three-month trip to Poland, the pastor had talked to me about a church in Billy-Montigny that was asking for a pastor. He thought I would be ideal because the congregation was made up of Polish immigrants and I spoke Polish. But I had been making so many trips into Poland and other East European countries that I told him I could not go.

"You know, they're still asking for a pastor. They're still waiting. They're desperate! Couldn't you at least visit them?"

"Well, I suppose I could." Inside I balked at the idea. A church pastorate would tie me down. How could I continue to make as many trips into Poland? And how could I think of expanding my ministry in Poland if I had the responsibility of a church? Besides, Billy-Montigny was located in the industrial, coal-mining area of northern France: dirty, sooty and drab compared to the lush green fields of Normandy.

Yet, I had to wonder. They had asked for me so many times, those hard-working Polish folk who needed a pastor. I remembered the close ties I had developed with the church members in Liège, and I realized that here, too, was an opportunity.

Perhaps they would have some insights that would be helpful as I continued my outreach into Poland. And, although the scenery would be bleak, the location nearer the Polish border would actually be better for my travels. I started to wonder if, maybe, God wanted me to go to Billy-Montigny, and I agreed to visit the church there.

About two weeks later I looked at the hopeful faces surrounding me: pleading faces fixed on mine and anxious for my response. I was meeting with the deacons and their wives in Billy-Montigny, discussing their church situation.

It was even worse than I had been led to believe. The former pastor, because of some moral problems, had been excommunicated by the church members. But, because the church building was in this pastor's name, he turned the tables a couple of weeks later and excommunicated the church! "If anyone wants to come to the meetings," he had said, "I am the pastor; I'm leading the services here!" His attitude divided the members. The deacons I was meeting with were from the splinter group that had left the church and was meeting in nearby Hénin-Beaumont at a Reformed church building they rented on Sunday afternoons. As I was thinking, one of the deacons turned to me and said, "Brother, we need you. Come and help us!"

What to do? In my heart I felt that I must help these people. But, at the same time, I was not ready to give them a definite answer. "Let's pray about it," I said. "I have to share this with my wife." Then I paused and asked, "Have you any money for another church building?"

One of the deacons replied, "All we have is thirty-five hundred French francs" (at that time, about seven hundred dollars).

With only 3,500 francs, they might as well have had nothing! "But how do you plan to expand? How can you purchase or build if you have no money?"

The spokesman scratched his head. "Well, there's a building—an old dance hall in the center of town—up for sale."

"How much do they want for it?"

"They want fifty thousand francs," I was told.

That was just over ten thousand dollars! My first reaction was one of disbelief: "How can you buy a building for fifty thousand francs if you only have thirty-five hundred in the treasury?" But as I looked around at their faces, features weathered by disappointment and yet still determined, I softened. "Well, perhaps it's the Lord's will. Let's pray, and we'll see. If you can get a church building and find a place for my family to live, I'll consider coming." We prayed together and I headed back to Calvados.

After I passed through the flat, coal-mining area with its slag heaps and heavily industrialized cities, the rolling hills of Normandy began to emerge on the horizon. For some reason, the situation in Billy-Montigny reminded me of the parable of the good Samaritan. I felt that the people I had just met were like the man in the ditch, beaten by robbers and bleeding. And here I was, passing by, and seeing the situation. I could easily be like the priest or the Levite and continue on past. After all, I had plenty to do in Calvados, and my circle of contacts in Poland was expanding all the time. Could I afford to tie myself down with a church? But the more I thought, the more I wondered whether I could afford not to. The situation in Billy-Montigny was desperate. They were discouraged. How could I leave them and just simply saunter past? They needed someone to care, someone to help them. In spite of all my misgivings, I began to pray, "Lord, do You want me in Billy-Montigny?"

My new friends in Billy-Montigny had told me to be sure to stop at Vimy Ridge, about six miles southwest of Billy-Montigny, on my way back to Calvados. In Vimy a memorial had been built to commemorate the sixty thousand Canadian young men who laid down their lives in order to liberate the area from Nazi occupation. Now the wind whipped through my summer clothes as I walked toward the huge stone memorial.

I had not expected the scene that met my eyes. The ridge set the memorial above the flat surrounding countryside, and trees were everywhere—not at all like the rest of Pas-de-Calais! Later I learned that a tree had been planted for each of the 11,285 Canadian soldiers who were missing in action.

The memorial itself is breathtaking: two immense stone figures that rise majestically from an enormous stone hemisphere. I felt antlike in comparison. The names of the 11,285 missing Canadian soldiers are etched into a wall surrounding the moument. On closer inspection, as I climbed the steps on one side of the hemisphere, I saw that the figures are women, weeping for the men they have lost.

I gazed in silence. Being Canadian, I felt a strange closeness to this place. And suddenly I thought, "If sixty thousand young Canadians were willing to die to liberate this part of France from the enemy, I should be willing to lay down my life—even bury myself here—to liberate these souls from Satanic power, which is much worse." A feeling of calm penetrated my soul, and I felt convinced that the Lord wanted me in Billy-Montigny.

The long drive to Calvados reminded me of my drives through Poland, and once again I wandered back in time. . . .

As I drove along the bumpy Polish road, I had to smile at the impression we were making. Cars were a rarity in Poland at that time, so people often stared at us. But today was truly a novelty because we were following a couple of hundred yards behind a militia jeep. For this reason, the townspeople must have thought we were "official," and as we threw tracts and Gospels of John from our car windows, nearly everyone dashed to pick them up!

As we reached the village's open market, I stuffed my pockets with tracts and got out to buy some fruit. After making my purchase, I handed the saleswoman a Polish tract without thinking much about it.

About twenty minutes later, as I was walking along the street in this same village, I felt a tug at my coattail. I turned around and looked down into the wrinkled face of an old peasant woman. The

dark shawl that she clutched around her shoulders did little to hide
her hunched back and crippled fingers. She held out a bony hand to
me as she asked, "Mister, can you give me a tract like you gave to
that lady where you bought the fruit?"

Had this crippled old lady followed me for twenty minutes for a
tract? Her simple earnestness stirred my heart, and I handed her one.
She took it eagerly and held it in both her hands as she read it. How
thankful she was for a simple gospel tract!

As my mind snapped back to the present, I wondered what
would happen to the thousands of people like that woman if I
took the church in Billy-Montigny. "Oh, Lord," I moaned, "I
love the Polish people. Must I give up my ministry with
them?" Suddenly I realized that the congregation in Billy-
Montigny was made up of Polish people, too.

"Thirty-five thousand francs? No, I'll never sell this building for that!" The thin French gentleman dangled a cigarette
from his right hand as he stared at us in astonishment.

I had been back in Calvados for a month and had rallied
the area churches behind me. I had collected gifts of money
and secured loans, so that when I returned to Billy-Montigny,
my funds, combined with what the congregation could
raise, totaled thirty-five thousand francs. "Let's make an offer
to the proprietor of that old dance hall," I suggested. "This is
the money that the Lord has provided for us! Let's see what
He's going to do with it." But the proprietor refused our offer.
He was still asking fifty thousand francs. So, we prayed—and
we waited.

A few weeks later, the proprietor came to us and said,
"Well, let's split the apple in two. I'll sell it for forty thousand
francs."

But I shook my head. "No, our final offer is thirty-five
thousand." Again we were forced to wait and pray. Finally,
after several weeks, the proprietor returned and agreed to our
offer. I phoned the treasurer. "Tell me exactly how much you
have in the treasury." I groaned when I learned we had only

37,650 francs. "This will never be enough to cover the lawyer's expenses—he'll want ten or fifteen percent of the price of the building." I paused. "Well, maybe he'll wait."

Finally the closing date was fixed: November 22, 1962. At six o'clock in the evening we were supposed to sign the papers for the old dance hall. The excitement in the air was almost tangible. For so many months the congregation had been waiting and praying for a miracle to happen—their own church building. And now it was about to transpire.

My heart was pounding as the lawyer discussed the sale, because I knew we would not have enough money. He shuffled through several papers, then looked at me. "Okay," he said finally, "I've figured your total cost."

I cleared my throat. "How much?"

He adjusted his glasses as he read the figure. "37,650 francs."

I looked over at the treasurer. His mouth was gaping. How could that figure be correct? Uneasily, I shifted my position and ran my hand through my hair as I turned to the lawyer. "That's a little lower than we expected."

He smiled kindly. "Well, the usual tax for this kind of transaction is ten percent of the purchase price, but since this is going to be a church building I charged only seven."

Then there was no mistake in the calculation! When the lawyer added his two-hundred-franc legal fee, the sum was 37,650 francs. And by "coincidence," the lawyer's figure was the exact amount of money we had, down to the last centime! For me, it was the finger of God, indicating His approval.

Since Billy-Montigny is located in the heart of a coal-mining area, most of the men in the congregation worked the mines six days a week. But the day after the closing, a Saturday, the congregation's coal miners took a day off from work to clean the building. The old dance hall became a buzz of dusting, sweeping, and scrubbing because we wanted to use it for our worship service the next day. There must have been a half-inch of dust over everything, since the building had been unused for five years. In fact, we found out later that the proprietor had been trying to sell the building for all those years. Nearly a hundred people had been interested, but the actual sale fell through each time. Once, a man made a down payment on the building, and the next day he died. His widow came to the owner and said, "We can't buy it!"

The more we heard, the more convinced we became that God had been reserving the building for us all along. I became even more convinced as the Lord blessed me with some special verses during my times of private Bible study. One morning, I was reading in the Book of Haggai. In the eighteenth verse of chapter two, I read; " 'do consider from this day onward, from the twenty-fourth day of the ninth month, from the day when the temple of the LORD was founded, consider.' " And more: "Then the word of the LORD came a second time to Haggai on the twenty-fourth day of the month saying, 'Speak to Zerubbabel governor of Judah saying, "I am going to shake the heavens and the earth. And I will overthrow the thrones of kingdoms and destroy the power of the kingdoms of the nations; and I will overthrow the chariots and their riders . . ." ' " (vv. 20–22).

Now, the average person reading this account might not be touched by these details, but, as I read, I realized that the dates mentioned were interesting "coincidences." Three times in that chapter of Haggai (in 2:10, 18, 20), the words *twenty-fourth day* are used. I thought back to my first contact with the church in Billy-Montigny. The twenty-fourth of September was when I first met with the deacons and told them that I would be willing to come if they could find a church building and a place for my family to live. When I arrived back in Calvados, Sophie said she would like to see Billy-Montigny and the old dance hall that the congregation was considering. And, as it happened, Sophie saw Billy-Montigny for the first time on October twenty-fourth. And now our first meeting in the new church building was scheduled for Sunday, the twenty-fourth of November! The promises of those verses in Haggai are tremendous. And to think that I should have come to Billy-Montigny for the first time on September 24, the second time

on October 24, and then to have our first meeting on
November 24, meant for me that the hand of God was
directing us.

What a day of celebration was the day we had our first
meeting in that old dance hall! From then on we had our work
cut out for us because we had to transform the building from
within. We had to rebuild the drinking bar into a library, the
dance hall into our sanctuary. We were able to recycle many of
the materials, and people volunteered to do the various jobs
that needed doing. We worked from November all through the
winter and spring.

I soon discovered that not only the church building was in
need of renovation, but the congregation as well. This work
was not easy, because in both cases we were trying to build out
of the ruins, and that is much more difficult than building a
new structure. Often I thought of the passage in Nehemiah
about the children of Israel rebuilding the walls of Jerusalem:
''And Judah said, The strength of the bearers of burdens is
decayed, and there is much rubbish; so that we are not able to
build the wall'' (Neh. 4:10 KJV). It is a tragic thing when a
church is destroyed from within, so that others must come and
try to clear out the rubbish and rebuild that which was ruined.

The transformation of the congregation was to be a long
process, but the church building was completed in a relatively
short time. By late May it was finished; we set the dedication
for June 3, 1963, the day of Pentecost that year. Hundreds of
people, some from Belgium and Normandy, planned to come
and celebrate with us.

A few weeks before the day arrived, I was reading in the Old
Testament again, and one verse came very forcefully to me.
''And this house was finished on the third day of the month
Adar, which was in the sixth year of the reign of Darius the
king. And the children of Israel, the priests, and the Levites,
and the rest of the children of the captivity, kept the dedication of this house of God with joy'' (Ezra 6:15–16 KJV). I could
scarcely believe my eyes that this house that Zerubbabel began
on the twenty-fourth day was finished and dedicated *on the*

third day! I had never noticed this verse before, and once again I felt the hand of God—even arranging the dedication of our church!

Soon I had settled into pastoring the Polish-French congregation in Billy-Montigny. Although my new responsibilities kept me very busy, my thoughts often wandered to Poland, and to the plans God had for me there. One morning, the memory of a special incident forced its way into my thoughts. . . .

I shifted uncomfortably in my seat. It was early morning and I had been traveling all night on the train from Warsaw to Vienna. Six of us shared a small compartment, including a middle-aged Polish woman who sat across from me. I felt in my soul that I must speak to her. I reached into my bag and pulled out my Polish Bible. Then I looked over at the woman. "Have you ever read the Bible?" I asked her in Polish.

She looked at me in surprise. "No, Have you got one?"

"Yes—" I began, but was interrupted as the woman spotted the Bible in my hand and her eyes grew wide in amazement. Suddenly she snatched it from me. She held it reverently, gazing at it a moment. Then she turned her wide, dark eyes on me. "All my life I've been looking for a Bible." In her excitement, the words tumbled out rapidly. "Could you sell this to me? How much do you want for it?" She began rummaging through her purse, still speaking. "I'll give you all the money I have for this Bible!"

"No, no," I replied, touching her arm to get her attention, "this is a gift for you."

She stopped her search and eyed me thoughtfully. Her next comment caught me completely off guard. "Why didn't you tell me last night that you had this Bible? I could have been reading it all night!"

I sighed. Why couldn't I just forget the people I had met in Poland? Why must their faces constantly return to haunt me? How many people in Eastern Europe were like that woman on the train? Or like the young girl sketching the Orthodox church? Did others have that same desire for a Bible? Was Christian literature still so scarce? My compulsion for meeting needs such as these had not waned as I began my pastoral duties in Billy-Montigny. If anything, it had become more intense. Time was slipping away. Something inside drove me to want to find new ways to help my friends behind the Iron Curtain. I knew there must be more I could do to respond to that terrific hunger for the Word of God.

7

One Little, Two Little, Three Little Bibles . . .

The Hungarian border sprawled before us. As I silently prayed, I hoped we had made the right decision. Having seen the lack of Bibles and Christian literature in Eastern Europe, I was especially moved by the even greater dearth of Scriptures in the Soviet Union. But the Soviet Union's borders were difficult to penetrate with large quantities of books, so I had tried to discover alternate means of providing the believers there with what they needed. I learned of Christians in some of the countries bordering the U.S.S.R. who were willing to transport Bibles across the border. One of these countries was Romania, which was our destination on this trip in mid-1969.

From France, the most direct route to Romania was through Austria and Hungary. And so I found myself on the Austrian-Hungarian border with a dear SGA brother and a station wagon packed to the gills with Bibles and Christian books. We had about 750 books inside the car and had piled them toward the front, camouflaging them as best we could. In the back we had our pillows, sleeping bags, food, camp stove, and other camping equipment.

We passed the initial passport inspection and arrived at customs control. Here a guard barked, "Open the back!" After I did so, he felt among our things, pushed around our camping paraphernalia, and then closed the back door.

"Open the side door!" he ordered next. At this I gulped. We had loaded the area between the two seats with bundles of books the height of the back seat. On top of the books we had only a deflated air mattress, folded and laid flat. The customs official bent down, propped his knee against the back seat, and ran his hand along the length of the air mattress. Then he climbed out, saluted us, and said, *"Auf Wiedersehen! Gute reise!"*

I could hardly believe my ears! Was he actually telling us we were free to enter the country? I climbed back into the car and said to John, my traveling partner, "We're like those two spies entering the land of Canaan. How could they not see those books?"

We traveled through Hungary that whole day, and all the way we were praying because we had one more border to cross—the one into Romania. The closer we came to it, the more nervous we became, and the tenser the atmosphere seemed between John and me. Finally, after dark, we arrived at the Romanian border. We could see about thirty cars ahead of us, and a sight that made our blood chill—half a dozen officials were checking every car.

I trembled like a leaf and said to John, "Close the window— I'm cold!"

As we waited, we began to claim all the promises of God that we could think of. At last our turn for inspection came. I got out and opened the back door. The Hungarian customs man put his hand under the pillows and between the boxes as if he knew where the books were. He pulled out a package of

Russian Bibles. "What's this?" he asked, holding the package in front of me.

The wonderful thing was that when he touched those Bibles, my fear and trembling ceased. Silently I prayed, "Oh, God, here we are discovered! Now I'm just anxious to know— how on earth are You going to get us out of this mess?" But aloud I answered the official: "Russian Bibles."

His eyebrows shot up. "Okay, unload the whole car."

Without argument we unloaded everything. We filled up several tables with our literature, and, of course, everyone crossing the border was curious to know what was going on! After we had emptied the inside of the car, an official came and stood looking up at the luggage rack we had on top. Three suitcases were strapped to it; two were John's and one was mine. He jerked his head in the direction of the rack, looked at me, and asked, "What do you have up there?"

"One," I replied. I meant "one suitcase" but hoped he would think I meant "one Bible" and would let us through.

Unfortunately I was wrong. "Take it down," he commanded.

I unstrapped and pulled down the huge suitcase, placed it on a table, and opened it. When the official saw its contents, he grabbed his head with both hands: the suitcase was stuffed with 150 New Testaments. "Bibles, Bibles, Bibles—everywhere, Bibles! I'm going to phone my director!" And he stalked off to one of the customs buildings.

I walked back to the car and sat down next to John. I shook my head. "John, we're in trouble here. We'd better phone *our* director!" While the official was gone, we began to pray.

In a few minutes the official was back, shaking his head. "This is illegal. You can't take any of this into Romania."

I replied, "I'm sorry, but I can't go in without Bibles. I've traveled two thousand kilometers [about 1,250 miles] and I must have Bibles with me."

"You can't do it," he said and walked away.

After he left, we kept on praying and waiting. In fact, we waited from 10:30 P.M. until 4:00 A.M. Finally I said, "Well, we have to do something!'' I picked up a few Russian Bibles from the table and headed toward the customs-control building, which the official had entered five and a half hours before.

One end of the building housed the Hungarian customs control; their Romanian counterparts were at the opposite end. As I entered the building I could hear the officials discussing our plight. The Hungarians were very stubborn; they did not want to let us through the border. The Romanians, on the other hand, appeared to be more understanding and were not set against us. In fact, they were almost begging the Hungarians to let us through! But the Hungarians kept refusing. I walked over to the Romanian side of the building and asked, "Well, will you let us into your country or not?"

A young official looked me up and down. "Leave your books, and then you can come in."

I shook my head. "No, we want to have our books with us."

"What have you got there?" he asked, gesturing toward the Russian Bibles I was carrying.

"Just Bibles. Everyone knows what the Bible is about. There's nothing wrong with the Bible."

"Let me see one!"

I handed him one of the Bibles and he showed it to his friends, who were playing cards because there was no traffic on the border at that hour of the morning. One of them read Russian. He took the Bible and browsed through it. After a while he looked up at me and said, "You know, this is a good book for Brezhnev and Kosygin, to get them converted. You come along with me."

He led me to the Hungarian side of the building and began to speak to one of the Hungarian officials. But the Hungarian kept shaking his head. He refused to budge. Finally the Hungarian guard turned to me and said, "Okay, bring everything into the office here."

John and I lugged all our stuff into the office. That Hungarian official unpacked every package, unwrapped every book, and checked every page. He put the books into piles according to their titles. Then he wrote down all the titles and counted every book. When he was finished, he took books from each pile and put them aside. I stood there trying to figure out what he was doing. Finally, after he had taken something from every pile, he pushed this new stack toward me and said, "Okay, take this and go!"

We nearly filled my large suitcase with the literature the Hungarian official allowed us to have—the suitcase that had held the 150 Russian Bibles! We put it in the car and drove into Romania. The rest of our literature remained on the border.

We found a small forest, drove into it, and stopped. We were so thrilled to have gotten into Romania at last! We began praying and thanked the Lord for His graciousness. Then I opened my Bible to the Gospel account of how Jesus required only five loaves and two fish to feed five thousand men. I turned to John and said, "Thank God for the few Bibles and books we were able to get through. God is surely able to multiply this and to bless thousands of people with just this one suitcase!"

As we sat praying and meditating, I said to John, "You know, we'll never get this job done, just the two of us trying to get literature into East Europe. Suppose we had a hundred people taking in a suitcase at a time? We could do much more than the two of us taking in seven hundred books at one time."

I began to envision a base in France—a depot stocked with thousands of Bibles, New Testaments, and Christian books for East Europe—where we could invite Christian young people from Canada, America, and England to come. We could call our base a launching pad, and each vehicle filled with literature would be a rocket armed with the gospel's power. My mind jumped from thought to thought. All that was left was to figure out how and where to start, and I was determined to do just that!

John and I slept soundly that night. The next day we delivered that suitcase of Bibles and Christian literature to a family who eventually delivered it to the Soviet Union. Three

days later we returned to the border. After our customs
inspection, the officials called us into the office where we had
left the bulk of our books. They had sealed them into twelve
cartons. We signed for them and left. We had all our books
back!

"Brother, how can you do anything for East Europe when
the doors are closed and the authorities are against you?" That
question echoed in my mind as I drove through the narrow
streets of Billy-Montigny, remembering that trip to Romania
and my dream of a launching pad for Christian literature. How
often similar versions of that question had been posed to me!
Having to answer it in deputation meetings encouraged me
somehow, because I realized afresh that it is the Lord's power
that enables *anything* to be done in His name!

Often I began to answer the question by turning to the
Revelation of John, where I read: " '. . . . He . . . who opens
and no one will shut, and who shuts and no one opens, says
this: "I know your deeds. Behold, I have put before you an
open door which no one can shut . . ." ' " (Rev. 3:7–8). "It's
not the government officials who have the keys to their
countries," I would continue. "It wasn't Mao Tse-tung who
had the key to his country, nor was it Stalin or Khruschev or
Brezhnev or even the authorities today. It's God who still has
the keys to every country and every situation."

Then I would relate another situation: when Peter was
locked behind the iron gate in prison: "And behold, an angel of
the Lord suddenly appeared, and a light shone in the cell; and
he struck Peter's side and roused him, saying, 'Get up
quickly. . . . Gird yourself and put on your sandals. . . . Wrap
your cloak around you and follow me' " (Acts 12:7–8). Now, of
course, Peter was worrying how they would ever penetrate the
iron gate! But the Bible continues: "And when they had passed
the first and second guard, they came to the iron gate that
leads into the city, *which opened for them by itself*; and they
went out . . ." (v. 10). "Well," I would say, "If God can open

the gates for Peter, I don't understand why we are worried about closed doors today into Eastern Europe. If God wants us to go in, He's going to open the gate!"

I smiled as my little Citroen jostled along, remembering another passage that had always interested me and had often served me well in meetings. This was the promise God made in Isaiah: "I will go before you and make the rough places smooth; I will shatter the doors of bronze, and cut through their iron bars" (Isa. 45:2). I would ask, "Couldn't the 'iron bars' be the Iron Curtain?" And the faces staring back at me would nod; at last seeming to comprehend.

I would continue, "Isn't it becoming clear that the *Lord* opens doors? Look what Paul tells the Corinthians: 'Now when I came to Troas for the gospel of Christ . . . a door was opened for me in the Lord' (2 Cor. 2:12). If God has promised, and He has done it for others, I don't see any reason why He will not open up doors for me and others in our mission."

As I continued driving toward the center of town, I was once again encouraged that the Lord was with me in my work to Eastern Europe—even though many kept telling me that I could do nothing because the doors to these countries were closed.

But what about the idea that the authorities and governments in Eastern Europe are against our work, and therefore that our hands are tied? I recalled a passage that I had once come across in the Book of Daniel. This, too, I often shared at deputation meetings. Nebuchadnezzar had had a dream that he could not understand. He found Daniel, and the Lord opened Daniel's understanding so that Daniel responded, "This sentence is by the decree of the angelic watchers, and the decision is a command of the holy ones, In order that the living may know that the Most High is ruler over the realm of mankind, and bestows it on whom He wishes, and sets over it the lowliest of men" (Dan. 4:17). And later even Nebuchadnezzar acknowledged that ". . . His dominion is an everlasting dominion, and His Kingdom endures from generation to generation. And all the inhabitants of the earth are accounted as nothing, but He does according to His will in the host of heaven and among the inhabitants of the earth; And no one can ward off His hand or say to Him, 'What hast Thou done?' " (vv. 34–35).

"God sets up these people in their places of authority and leadership," I would say. "They're not there by accident. Satan didn't put those people there. *God* put those people there! From the time I first read this passage, I've tried not to question the wisdom of God—why God has allowed so many countries and so many millions of people to be under the dominion and reign of the hammer and sickle. 'No one can ward off His hand.' And no one can say to God, 'What are you doing?' Who am I to question God's wisdom for allowing such men as are in power in Eastern Europe? God put them there, and He certainly has a plan and a purpose for it. Once this became clear in my mind, then I could say, 'Okay, now we can work and trust God to open the doors and give us favor with these men who are in power in these countries.' When God decides to open a country, no man can oppose God. Man cannot thwart God's purposes!"

As my hands gripped the steering wheel, I reflected on how many times my faith had been tested. The Lord had given me several instances to learn that He, indeed, has the power to open or close the Iron Curtain, although sometimes I did wonder at His timing and just what He was trying to teach me. One incident was particularly memorable. . . .

The bedroom clock's incessant ticking was becoming etched on my brain. In frustration I threw back the covers and flicked on the light switch: 2:30 A.M. I turned off the light and drew the covers around me once again. As the clock continued to tick, I tossed and turned, unable to sleep. I could not seem to shake my nervousness. *Why* was Andrew's Polish visa denied? This was one trip I did not want to make alone.

For three days, Andrew Daneliuk (an SGA co-worker) and I had been waiting in Vienna for his Polish visa to be processed. We had 250 Russian New Testaments that we planned to deliver to Poland.

The Christians in Poland would know how to get them into the Soviet Union. But, after those three days, Andrew's application for a visa to Poland was denied. So I was faced with the dilemma of having to travel to Poland by myself.

Just thinking of the trip made me uneasy. Because of the crisis in the Middle East the tension at East European borders was intense. I had a brand-new car and, because of the mounting turmoil, realized that, should my literature be discovered, my car would probably be confiscated and I could be put into prison. I dozed fitfully, hardly refreshed when dawn's rays announced the arrival of a new day.

By late afternoon, though, I was on my way. I had filled my trunk with used clothes for Poland and stashed the New Testaments under the floor pad between the two seats of my car. The books were barely hidden and would not be hard to miss, but I reasoned that if I could reach the border sometime late at night, there might be less chance of investigation by the guards.

The sight that met my eyes at the Czech border was anything but encouraging. From behind the windshield, all I could see were electrified barbed wire fences patrolled by soldiers with fierce-looking German shepherds. The atmosphere was bristling, as if a state of war existed.

As I drove into the border compound, the Czech officials opened my trunk and saw that it was loaded with clothes. They asked me to close it and told me they had to seal it so that I would not open it in Czechoslovakia. To my amazement, the rest of my border inspection was minimal, and I was able to pass into the country for transit to Poland.

By 9:00 P.M. I was at the Polish border. Just ahead of me was a bus with about fifty people aboard. In what seemed a very short time, they were processed and on their way. "Well," I thought, "it's late. Maybe they'll let me go through without any problems."

I inched my car to the first checkpoint and showed my passport. A steel-faced official studied it in silence. Then he turned to me. "Mr. Kapitaniuk, do you have any literature?"

His question struck me like a thunderbolt. I had never before been asked such a question on the Polish border! For a few seconds I was dazed and didn't know what to say. Then, collecting myself, I looked the official straight in the eye. "Yes, I have some."

The official frowned. "What have you got?"

"Oh, a few Bibles." My heart was pounding, but I tried to act as nonchalant as possible. I hoisted my big suitcase from the car and opened it. Right on top were my English Bible and my Polish Bible. The guard started to take everything out, including some books by Watchman Nee. "Excuse me, sir," I quickly interjected, "but I need my Polish Bible. I've been invited to speak in the Polish churches." As I spoke, I pulled the official letter of invitation from the president of the Evangelical Union from my pocket. I handed it to the official. In this letter the president said, "Mr. Kapitaniuk, could you come and visit our churches and minister to our Christians?"

The official paused just long enough to scan the letter. But he seemed to read and not understand. "You have no right to bring any books into the country," he responded in Russian.

I was tired and was growing frustrated. "Why not?" I blurted.

The official gazed at me thoughtfully, his eyes narrowed. Then he spoke, again in Russian. "We have orders from the Kremlin to find out who's bringing Russian literature into Poland, because a lot of it is getting from Poland into Russia."

My heart felt like it was jumping from my chest as I stood rooted to the spot. I thought to myself, *Well, I know who they're looking for!* I asked no more questions, and the guard continued his search. When he had cleaned out all the literature in my suitcase, he turned to me. "Do you have any more literature?"

I thought quickly and said, "Yes." As I did so, I handed him my briefcase. In it were more books, some tracts, and some addresses. So many times I had traveled to Poland with no problems; I never dreamed they would check me so thoroughly! They went through my briefcase with a fine-tooth comb and cleaned out every little piece of paper I had.

For the third time the official turned to me and asked, "Have you got any more literature?"

By now my heart was in my throat. Years before I had resolved that I would never lie at a border when traveling into Eastern Europe. But what could I do? What could I say? To say, "No, I don't have any more," would be a lie, because there were still over two hundred New Testaments in my car. But to say, "Yes, there's more"—I hated to think what would happen, knowing now that they were hunting for me and others who dared to bring Russian Bibles into Poland.

For some reason, I decided to say nothing, to simply ignore the question. Surprisingly the guard did not press for an answer. He took everything he had found and walked away. I breathed a sigh of relief and whispered, "Thank You, Lord!"

But my respite was short-lived. I saw the official coming back toward me. "Okay," he announced as he got closer, "now I'm going to search your car."

I froze. In a flash I saw that if he discovered those New Testaments, I would lose everything. Not only would the literature be confiscated, but also the car, and I would either have to pay a heavy fine or be imprisoned. Desperately, I began to pray that God would intervene and do a miracle for me and blind the guard's eyes to the literature.

The official searched the trunk and then moved to the back seat. He patted from the top down, then came to the seat and, next, to the floor pad. My heart nearly stopped as he slapped the floor pad a few times and I thought, "Well, here I go!"

But the guard kept moving. He started feeling the front seat. Then he opened the glove compartment and moved some things around in there. And then—was I seeing right?—he walked away! I felt as though I had just been through a wringer. My heart was still pounding, my hands were sweating, my mind was reeling. But God had preserved me!

By now it was 10:00 P.M. and very dark. As I stood waiting, I silently praised the Lord for His protection. Suddenly, the official was by my side once more. He was holding something in his hand. "What's this?" he demanded, frowning. He was holding a small red booklet. The title was in English: *The Christian's Answer to the Jehovah's Witnesses.* I looked at the official and said, "This is a book that I'm bringing to Poland to get it translated and printed. It exposes the false teachings of the Jehovah's Witnesses."

Without a word, he turned and walked away.

Again I stood in the dark, waiting. The minutes seemed to drag by.

Finally the official emerged from the building, carrying an armload of something. As he came nearer, I could not believe my eyes, for in his arms he held all my literature—all my books, Bibles, and tracts. He put the whole load on the hood of my car, saluted me, and said, "Good-bye; good trip!"

Only later, as I thought things through, did I realize what had happened. The Polish government is battling the Jehovah's Witnesses and many of them are in prison. During that time the Jehovah's Witnesses were outlawed in Poland (only recently have they been allowed to register). The government was against them because they refused to enter the army (as conscientious objectors) and because they had secret underground presses that distributed a good deal of literature. Evangelicals, on the other hand, were registered, operated legally, and were even allowed to print literature, with certain government stipulations.

In the minds of the Polish authorities, I was helping their cause, because that little red book exposed the false teachings of the Jehovah's Witnesses and would help the authorities undermine this illegal church. Somehow, in the midst of all my jumble of books, God provided that little tract—just what I needed.

I left the border and drove till I found a secluded spot. Then I pulled my car off the road and had a terrific time thanking the Lord for the way He had protected me, the literature, and my car. I also made another prayer. "Lord," I said, "this was too painful an experience. Only You know what I just lived through; I couldn't bear it another time. If you want me to take literature into Eastern Europe, I'm not going to hide it; I'm going to take it and trust You to get me through. . . ."

I stared at the paper before me. "Are you sure there's no mistake?" I asked. The year was 1970. I'd stopped by the Polish consulate for what was usually a routine procedure— picking up a Polish visa. But something wasn't right. "Maybe you have the name wrong. It's Kapitaniuk, K-a-p-i-t. . . ."

The official on the other side of the counter shifted uncomfortably. "No, sir, there's no mistake. Your Polish visa has been denied."

"But why?" I implored gently. "Did they tell you why? Did they give you a reason?"

A muscle twitched in the official's face. I had been to this consulate several times for visas, and he knew me. As our eyes met, he looked quickly at the floor. "Your visa has been denied by order of the Polish government."

"And they gave you no reason?"

He looked at me, said nothing, and shrugged.

I looked again at the paper I held in my hands. I had filled out countless such forms before, but none had come back like this one. Stamped in bold letters that stretched across my application were the words *persona non grata*.

I folded the application and stuffed it into my jacket pocket. Silently, I nodded to the official, turned, and strode out of the room. What did they mean, *persona non grata*? How could I be an unwelcome person?

About two years had passed since the tract about the Jehovah's Witnesses eased my trip to Poland with the Russian New Testaments. I had made several other trips since then, to Poland and to several other East European countries as well, including the Soviet Union. Between these trips, I still pastored the church in Billy-Montigny and was heavily involved in the pastoral duties. And, in addition, my family was rapidly expanding. Sophie and I now had six sons: Daniel (thirteen), Philippe (ten), David (nine), Paul (seven), Joël (four), and a newborn, Jean.

I had never had visa problems before. Why now?

Perhaps someone in Poland had mentioned my literature activities to the Soviet authorities. I smiled and shook my head. What difference would that have made? I had already been stopped three times at the Russian border with Christian literature. Then, as I thought about it, I realized that could indeed have made a difference. Perhaps the Soviet authorities were not pleased with my literature involvement and had pressured the Polish government to deny me a visa. If this were true, how long would it last? A month? A year? Three years?

"I will go before you . . . and cut through their iron bars."
The Lord was apparently not cutting through any iron
bars right now. Here I was in France, but my heart was in
Poland! If I could not travel there, what could I do? What
about the people there, the need for literature—and yet, even
as I questioned, I knew that man could not thwart God's
purposes. The Lord had His reasons for not allowing me to
travel to Poland right then.

Unexpectedly, my trip to Romania flashed through my
mind again. Especially the idea for a "launching pad." *A
launching pad!* I had been so busy traveling that I had not
given the idea much thought. But now I would be stuck in
France for who knew how long. Maybe I couldn't go to Poland,
but the Lord knew of other ways to meet the spiritual needs of
Eastern Europe, and I knew He would show them to me.

8

Operation Launch Pad

Here it comes! Here it comes!" a small boy announced excitedly as he ran alongside the mobile chapel I was maneuvering through the narrow streets of Hénin-Beaumont. Children came running from all directions as I inched the huge trailer truck around a corner and into a small vacant lot.

I stepped down from the cab and was immediately surrounded by eager little French faces all trying to talk at once. "That's some fancy truck you have there!" "Are you going to show a movie today?" "How long is it?" "Is it really about savages?" "My sister says it's free—is that true?"

Laughingly I answered their questions as my sons and I prepared to show the movie. I had had no idea there were so many children in Hénin-Beaumont! Most were quite young, but I noticed several teenagers leaning against a nearby apartment building and watching indifferently. I prayed that they would come closer, once the film began.

As I surveyed the growing crowd I glanced up at one of our brightly colored posters tacked to one of the lower windows in the mobile chapel:

COME TO THE FILM!!!

COME TO THE FILM!!!

IT'S FREE!!! IT'S FREE!!!

Thursday afternoon, our mobile chapel
will be in your neighborhood
(meet in the vacant lot at 15 H)
to show the film *Peace Child*,
an unforgettable story of primitive jungle
treachery in the 20th century, and how
God's Peace Child brought true peace to the
Sawi people of Netherlands New Guinea.
Everyone is welcome.
Don't miss it!

COME TO THE FILM!!!

COME TO THE FILM!!!

An artist friend painted this poster—oil paint on a shiny tin plate—and it had been effective. It galled me to think how much money the print shop downtown would want to print posters such as this! In my opinion, the price we had paid for just a few simple tracts was outrageous. But as I looked at the children around me, I realized that anything we spent would be worth it. At least we had the money and the materials to print things when we needed them. How different it was for my friends in Poland. My mind took me back in time again. . . .

"Are you allowed to print in this country?"

A dozen pairs of eyes watched me, not as warily as they had the year before, but still cautious. It was 1958, and I had just concluded a trip through Poland and was meeting with the Central Committee of the Evangelical Union in Warsaw. The middle-aged chairman spoke: "Yes."

I frowned, confused. So many people had badgered me for literature! "Then why don't you print?"

He smiled sadly and raised his hands in resignation. "We don't have the men, and we don't have the money."

So, *that* was the problem! Now that I knew, I could take action. "Listen, I'll make a deal with you. *You* get the men; *I'll* get the money."

On my next trip to Poland, I brought in several tracts and booklets for my Polish brothers to translate and print. But then came the dilemma: "We don't have the paper; we'll have to import it."

Why import the paper? My friends explained that Poland had a paper shortage. Often the church was prevented from printing Bibles and Christian books, not for lack of permission, but for lack of paper. Well, what seemed a predicament to my friends was almost a relief to me! If they could obtain permission to print, I felt sure we could provide the paper. I wrote SGA headquarters and explained that if we could provide the paper, our brothers could print inside of Poland.

Christians in America, when alerted by SGA, provided the money for the printing of those first tracts. After the tracts came a major project: *The Pilgrim's Progress* had just been translated into Polish. While I was in Canada on furlough, I received a telegram from Warsaw: "Brother, we need three tons of paper immediately to print *The Pilgrim's Progress.*" Once again, Christians in Canada and the United States provided the money for the three tons of paper, and my friends were able to print their first edition of John Bunyan's classic in the late 1950s.

From then on, we encouraged the Christians in Poland to print as much as they could. SGA provided the paper; some years we provided as much as forty tons! Even so, there was never enough Christian literature for the Polish people. And the situation in Poland was gradually changing. Within a few years it was difficult for the Polish Christians to obtain ink and, soon after that, to find the necessary plates for their offset presses. Once the Polish government lifted my travel restrictions, I believed I would find a way to provide my friends in Poland with more literature. . . .

A nudge from my son Daniel brought me back to reality and reminded me that it was time to start the movie. The children had filled the trailer to capacity. Everyone chattered excitedly as I pushed through the throng toward the projector. But, as I did so, I glanced out the back window. A large group of

sad-eyed youngsters stood clustered behind the trailer, straining for a glimpse; the chapel simply could not hold everyone. I opened the window and said that we would show the film again, that everyone would have a chance to see it. I noticed that several of the teenagers I had seen earlier were standing on the fringe of this group, and I offered up a silent prayer of thanks.

Once the film began, the children settled down and were soon engrossed in the story. I had to shake my head in disbelief; I was actually surrounded by French children watching a gospel film! Such things didn't normally happen in France! In addition, only six short months before, this trailer, rusted almost beyond repair, had been sitting on a trash heap. Yet even then, I had seen the potential for outreach. . . .

"What are you going to do with this old thing?" I asked.

The huge twenty-ton trailer must have been an impressive piece of machinery in its time. From the faded lettering and picture on the outside, I saw that it had been used for advertising wine. Inside was a refrigerator and a tap for running water. This truck must have traveled all over France, but now it sat, crumbling and useless, in a Paris junkyard.

"Well, it's been sitting here for five years. We want to junk it." Gaston Loret, the junkyard owner, was a short, muscular fellow who loved the Lord and was a good friend of mine. He was also a millionaire and gave thousands of dollars to God's work around the world. He had built an orphanage in India and bought a movie theater in Paris and transformed it into a church.

"Brother, may I have it? I'd like to show Moody science films in it."

Gaston raised his bushy black eyebrows in surprise. "If you can make use of it, go ahead; take it!"

"Making use of it" proved to be more difficult than I had anticipated. The first major difficulty was getting the trailer to Billy-Montigny. My brother-in-law George, a truck driver, returned to Paris with me a few days later. He helped me start the engine, inflate the tires, and maneuver the forty-five-foot tractor-trailer onto the street. We did fine until we came to the first corner; as we took the turn, we hooked a classy French sports car parked by the side of the road. As I hopped down from the cab and surveyed the damage, I groaned; the fender of that flashy car had disappeared into the body of our big trailer. But, to my amazement, when George backed the truck out, the car's fender was not even dented. Our trailer was too rusted to do any damage!

And that was only the beginning of our "exodus." The motor kept stalling, the tires went flat, one of the radiator hoses burst, and our engine overheated. What should have been a simple two-hour drive turned out to be an eleven-hour marathon. We left Paris about three o'clock in the afternoon and pulled into Billy-Montigny at two o'clock the following morning!

Then we had to decide how to get our "new" acquisition repaired. The engine had obvious problems, and the basic shell was badly eaten by rust and needed significant body work. I phoned Operation Mobilization's headquarters in Zaventem, Belgium, since I knew they did work of this type.

"Bring it over," was the reply.

George and I hardly looked forward to another eleven-hour drive in that vehicle! But, to our relief, we had no major problems until we arrived in Brussels, about three miles from Zaventem. Here we stalled and could not restart the motor. Servicemen from a nearby garage responded quickly to our phone call; they found an electrical short that was draining our battery. They got the truck started and, with a prayer, we ventured onto the road once again. As we crept toward our destination, the lights grew dimmer and dimmer. Just as we pulled into the parking lot of the OM headquarters in Zaventem, the motor and the lights went out completely. I smiled at George. "Well, thank God, we're here!"

The next day I met with Frank Bus, the garage foreman of OM. When he caught sight of our truck, he turned to me in amazement. "What can we do with this monster?" He shook his head as he looked it up and down. "You go and pray for a couple of hours. And I'll have to pray here and think. Then we'll decide."

I went into a nearby building and prayed earnestly that the Lord would move these people to help us. Just before noon I came out and asked, "Well, what did the Lord say to you?"

He grinned. "We'll help you get that thing repaired!"

For six months we worked with OM personnel, slapping that trailer into shape. We completely remodeled it. We put on new sheet-metal sides and covered the rusted-out areas with tin. We tore out and replaced the rotted interior. Finally, the work was completed, and we drove our remodeled mobile chapel back to France.

Already it had been a wonderful means of showing gospel films and of proclaiming a Christian witness in our own community. The children watching *Peace Child* today were only a few of the hundreds who would be touched by our mobile-chapel films. I rejoiced that at least the denial of my Polish visa had not thwarted my French ministry.

But my heart still ached for Poland. What was happening there while I was temporarily tied to Western Europe? Was there nothing I could do for Eastern Europe while I waited for the Polish authorities to reverse their decision about me?

Strangely enough, the mobile chapel became the means not only for reinvolving me in direct outreach to Eastern Europe, but for fulfilling the vision I had first had in Romania. That dream—of a "launching pad" for Christian literature—first began to take tangible shape when I noticed an apparently unused tract of land. . . .

"Do you know who owns that land?" I asked, pointing.

I stood near my French neighbor's small garden plot as he weeded a row of lettuce. Shielding his eyes from the sun, he looked in the direction I had indicated. Then he frowned up at me. "Why?"

"I'd like to buy it."

He shook his head. "The coal mines own that land. Many people have tried to buy it, but the mines refuse to sell. You don't have a chance."

"Well, I can try." The land certainly didn't look like much; it was covered with rubbish of every kind—old mattresses, refrigerators, and rusty car parts. But the property was long and I knew it would be perfect for our mobile chapel. The trailer's great bulk had been a problem from the start; there was simply no place to park it in Billy-Montigny, where parking lots were tiny. Every time I found a spot, the police would say to me, "Take this out of here; it's hindering traffic." The situation was becoming desperate.

Another pressing circumstance was our apartment, which was damp and drafty. This caused innumerable health problems for the children, and our family was growing besides. Sophie and I needed a bigger place, and I had been looking for a good location on which to build.

In addition, the "launching pad" vision was fresh in my mind, as I had recently returned from Romania. I wanted a piece of land where we could build a place to store literature and vehicles, and perhaps build a youth center. Since this property looked ideal, I approached the mine officials to see whether they were willing to sell me the land. As I entered the office, I saw a man I knew, Monsieur Volka.

My spirits rose at seeing this man, because both of us had been involved in an interesting incident some months earlier. A girl in our neighborhood who had been born with multiple deformities had achieved world attention when her photo hit the major newspapers. A British journalist arrived to do research on the girl, because his journal was offering to finance special surgery in America to try to correct the deformities.

This journalist could speak no French, so he asked me to be his interpreter for several days as he interviewed the girl and made arrangements for her to go to the States. This involved meeting all the town officials, including M. Volka. After the operation, when the girl returned to France, a special reception was prepared. The journalist returned, I interpreted for him again, speeches were made, medals were awarded. Because of the part I had played, I was awarded a medal for distinguished service to the town of Billy-Montigny. Throughout the whole saga, M. Volka, chief engineer in the central office of the coal mines, was one of the town-council members I had gotten to know quite well.

He recognized me at once. "What can I do for you?" he asked.

"Monsieur Volka, I need some help; I need land. Can the coal mines sell me a piece of land?"

"What do you want it for?"

"For several things. I need to build a house for my family, and I need a place to put our mobile chapel. Perhaps, eventually, we'll also want to develop a youth and children's ministry."

He nodded. "Those are good reasons. But we don't have any land."

"What about that piece at rue Diderot?" I ventured.

He thought for a moment. "We haven't considered selling that piece of land. But I could inquire in Paris."

"Thanks. I'd appreciate that." I left the office and began praying that the coal mines would sell us that tract of land.

Four months later I received a letter from M. Volka. "Yes, we can sell that land. You can buy all or part of it." This was cause enough for rejoicing, but I was amazed when I read the price they wanted for it: twenty-two francs for the first ninety feet from the main road, and six francs ten centimes per square yard for the rest of the plot. At that time this meant about $1.80 per square yard of land. What a terrific bargain in a country where land could cost many, many times that! A huge lot of land—100 feet wide and 600 feet long (about 1 1/2 acres) —for $12,000 was totally unexpected.

But I didn't have $12,000, so I couldn't answer. I wrote letters to America. I visited Great Britain. We prayed and waited. But no money came.

One day George Verwer, founder of OM, invited me to speak at a conference in Paris. While there I decided to ask my friend Gaston Loret for a loan. My idea was to buy the land, wait a few years, and then resell part of it at a higher price and repay him. I explained this to him.

"This is American speculation. I'm not interested." He paused, staring at me with his penetrating dark eyes. "But if you'd be interested in going into business with me, I'm ready."

"What business?"

"A secondhand car-and-parts business. I'm a bachelor, and I pay a lot of income tax. But you have a big family, many children. If we formed a company together, we wouldn't have to pay so much income tax. Then we could use this money to develop God's work."

It sounded logical and I agreed immediately. But the Lord would soon show me that He had other ideas.

Gaston came to see the land and was very happy with it. It was ideal for a big garage where we could resell parts that he had overstocked in Paris. So he came up with the $12,000 and we bought the land. After having lived in Europe for eighteen years, now, in 1970, I was a landowner!

Just before I left for a brief furlough in the States, I received word that the Christians in Poland desperately needed ten tons of paper. So I visited Back to the Bible Broadcast headquarters in Lincoln, Nebraska, where Theodore Epp asked me to record two five-minute tapes about the Polish Christians' need for paper. I made the tapes and left. Two months later I was in Chicago, preparing to return to France, when I had a phone call from Mr. Epp. He was exuberant. "Brother," he said, "we have your money for the ten tons of paper for Poland—ten thousand dollars."

His enthusiasm was contagious and, as my plane headed back for France, my mind reeled with the ideas I had for Eastern Europe, especially the "launching pad." One thing we needed desperately was literature. I wrote to a mission in Denmark, but they had no Bibles to offer. However, they gave me the address of a Swedish mission, which I contacted. The Swedish mission responded, "Yes, we have Bibles in several East European languages; they cost between $1.50 and $2.00 apiece."

I wrote back, explaining our plans for outreach to Eastern Europe and added, "We recently bought some land and are just beginning to build our storage garage. We haven't any money, but we need Bibles."

A second letter soon arrived from Sweden. In the letter was a list: 25,000 Russian Bibles, 25,000 Ukrainian Bibles, 25,000 Bulgarian Bibles, and 25,000 Polish Bibles—a total of 100,000 Bibles. "These are our gift to you," the letter read.

With a jolt I realized that not one penny had come in from my new business with Gaston—our business had not even been established—and yet I had ten tons of paper and 100,000 Bibles! *God is certainly working things out differently than I'd planned!* I thought.

But the Lord wanted to be sure I understood that *He* was providing. A few days later I received a letter from Gaston Loret. "Brother Kapitaniuk," it said, "I feel that God doesn't want me in the business world anymore; I have to quit and go into some kind of spiritual ministry. So, I'm no longer interested in forming a partnership with you. If you can pay me back the money I invested, you can do whatever you want with the land."

Gaston's letter caught me by surprise. From Paris he had already shipped me a six-ton truck, a back-hoe tractor, and an electric cement mixer to begin clearing and building for our business venture. Now, in an instant, our plans had been dissolved.

But, as I reflected on the situation, I was far from gloomy; in fact, an excitement began to bubble up within me. I realized that this was the Lord's way of providing for us. It was like a dream—we had the land and all the equipment we needed to build. We did not even have to use part of the land for secular business; it could all be used for expansion of our French work and outreach to Eastern Europe.

For the next five years, we built: a youth center, a large garage/storage building, and a new house for my family. The house was built by a general contractor, but we did the rest of the work ourselves with materials we either obtained free or for very low prices. Gaston allowed me to pay him a nominal price for the truck, back hoe, and cement mixer.

By 1973 we had obtained some vehicles and had made preparations for sending our first organized shipment of literature behind the Iron Curtain. My dream for Operation Launch Pad was about to become reality.

"Lord, if they get through those borders with all those books and Bibles, I'll take it as a sign that You're with us in this venture." I watched as the two vehicles, each loaded with half a ton of Christian literature, turned a corner and went out of sight.

Was my Romanian vision taking form at last? All our preparations had been leading up to this moment—all our sweating and building and planning. Suddenly I felt very insecure. How could they possibly get through with that much literature? Had we done the right thing? I felt a great need for encouragement and prayer. I rushed off and sent telegrams to churches across Canada and the States: "Two rockets fully loaded left the base for Eastern Europe. Pray for safe deliveries."

We waited several days, because France is quite a distance from Eastern Europe. I wondered how our friends were faring. Had they gotten through? Had they delivered the materials? Each day I fervently prayed that the Lord would grant His favor in this new outreach.

I will never forget the day we saw those vehicles returning! They pulled into the yard, and the drivers hopped out and rushed over to us. They were singing and praising God. In between their praises and hugs, they cried, "We got through! We delivered the goods!" One of the young men looked at me and said, "Brother Kapitaniuk, when we left this base a few days ago, we fasted and prayed until we delivered the books to their destination. Only then did we take food."

To me, the safe delivery of this initial shipment was the stamp of approval that God was with us in this new endeavor. And it was only the beginning of a program of literature delivery that continued every summer for many years.

During those summers our teams of British and American young people crossed East European borders with thousands of Bibles, Scripture portions, Christian books, and other longed-for material. It dawned on me that if my visa to Poland (and later to other East European countries) had not been denied, the "launching pad" vision would probably never have been realized. Through my inability to travel, the Lord had enabled thousands of pieces of literature to reach behind the Iron Curtain. My immobilization was God's way of nudging me to establish an outreach that stretched far beyond my own capabilities!

Although the five years I was denied travel into Poland were frustrating, I could indeed see the Lord's hand at work in spite of the circumstances. My ministry in France was becoming well established; the Polish-French congregation where I served as pastor had by now settled into the new church building. Operation Launch Pad was in full swing. In the newly built youth center, we began a children's Bible club with the neighborhood French children. And the mobile chapel provided a way to present the gospel to an even wider audience.

Yet I ached for an opportunity to do more for Poland. How long would my visa be denied? Was my personal ministry there over?

No, the Lord was not finished with me yet. In fact, my outreach to Poland was only beginning. As I chafed in my limitations, I failed to see that the Lord had noted my desire and had already begun to set in motion the opportunity I longed for. Once again it was the mobile chapel that He used as the instrument; it initiated an operation that I could never have conceived in my wildest dreams, one that would enable me to reach thousands more Poles than I ever thought possible.

9

"That Also Which This Woman Has Done Shall Be Spoken of . . ."

Stretching my legs, I pushed my chair from the table and sighed contentedly. Once again Sophie had proven her culinary artistry. And that day we had the honor of sharing that artistry with two brothers from England. One of our visitors worked as a foreman in the printing department of a bank. At a pause in the conversation, he turned to me and remarked, "You know, we're liquidating a lot of our old machinery."

His offhand statement caught my attention. For a long time I had envisioned a simple press that we could use to print the posters and tracts we needed for our mobile chapel ministry. The prices we paid at our local print shop were phenomenal, and we needed to find a cheaper way to print our material. I looked eagerly at our visitor. "You wouldn't have an old press I could use, would you?"

He smiled. "Sure, we've got one. We'll see to it that you get it."

Some time later, as we unpacked the crates, sawdust and pieces of machinery formed piles around our feet. I had to pinch myself—we had a printing press at last!

Assembling the press was not difficult, but then the fun began—how did it run? Although I had never printed anything in my life and didn't know the first thing about it, I wasn't concerned. I had learned most things by doing. Why should printing be any different?

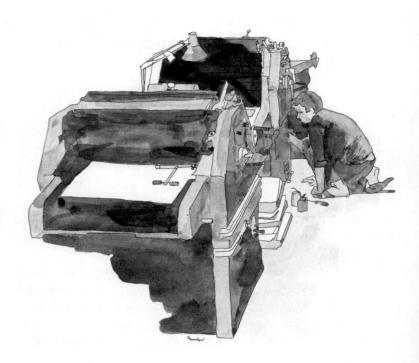

I was so wrong! The press seemed to be assembled properly but, even though we tried everything, our efforts ended in frustration. When I realized that we weren't going to make it work, I contacted a printer friend who came and had it running in no time. But, as soon as he left, the press refused to cooperate.

It was the rare machine that I could not fix. Whenever anything in the house needed repairing—a plumbing fixture, an appliance, a piece of furniture—I could usually do the job. If I didn't know what to do at first, I would learn what needed to be done in the process of repairing whatever was broken. Why couldn't I get this press to work? I had tried everything! A press would be so helpful to us. I wondered why the Lord even allowed us to get it if it was only going to sit useless.

Then I smiled as I remembered another time some years before when I was also completely at a loss to fix something. Surely the Lord would help us now, just as He had provided exactly what I needed then. . . .

A bony elbow dug deeper and deeper into my ribs as I tried to drive. How we had managed to squeeze nine people into my tiny car I will never know! As we jostled over the dirt road, my ability to steer decreased with every swerve I made to avoid the numerous rocks and potholes. I could barely move my arms. With each bump, we would leap into the air for a second, only to land with the telltale thud of an overloaded car. I found myself continuously praying for patience and endurance. I glanced at the man next to me and he smiled warmly. For a moment I forgot my discomfort and thanked the Lord for the chance to travel in Poland with these dear people.

I had just deposited Sophie and the children at her relatives' home in Zapalow. Then, in Przemysl, I had picked up eight passengers who wanted to accompany me to an evening meeting in a little village about thirty miles away, just west of the Russian border. But I had had no idea that the road would be so bad. The further we traveled, the more bumps and ruts we hit. At one point the road got so bad that I had to slow down to a crawl. As I did so, I heard a rock hit something underneath the car, but I didn't give it a second thought.

I breathed a sigh of relief as we finally pulled up in front of the wooden country house where the meeting was to be held.

As we piled out of the car, the villagers came to greet us. The warm summer evening lent an aura of calm as I talked with the gathering people. Suddenly a young man rushed up to me, his eyes wide. "Brother Kapitaniuk, the oil is pouring out of your car!"

The calm shattered, I dashed to my car, followed by the rest of the throng. I remembered the rock we had hit and realized with dismay that the bump must have split the crankcase. One of the Polish men reached the car before I did. He was trying to plug the hole with a knife and an old rag when I arrived. But his efforts were in vain; soon the ground underneath my car was a dark, shiny pool. Helplessly we stared in silence as the oil completely drained from my car.

As I watched the last few drops of oil dripping to the ground, my mind raced. What would I do now? Here I was in no-man's-land with a cracked crankcase and no oil. How would I let Sophie know what had happened? How could I get the car fixed, since the part I needed simply didn't exist in Poland? How could I put this dilemma from my mind and preach what my brothers and sisters needed to hear? How would Sophie and the children and I continue our Polish itinerary? How would I transport the car out of the country for repairs? I was miles from civilization—or, at least, from any civilization that could help me. Oh, Lord! Oh, Lord!

While I stood brooding I felt a hand on my shoulder. I looked into the face of a young man, one of the group that had ridden with me from Przemysl. "Brother," he said, "you go have your meeting. I'll try to repair your car."

"*You're* going to repair it?" I asked doubtfully. I looked him up and down. Was he even twenty?

"I'll try."

I scrutinized his eager face. How could he possibly repair the huge crack in the crankcase? This was a foreign car and would need a special part, which he could never find in Poland—especially out in the country. I sighed and shook my head as I realized this problem was beyond me. And how could a mere Polish youth, with few resources at his disposal and probably very little experience, effect the miracle that my car needed?

At the same time, I had no choice but to let him try. And there was always the outside chance that he might succeed! At least he was willing to make an attempt. I turned to him with a forced grin. "Well," I said, running a nervous hand through my hair, "if you can do it, the Lord bless you, because I don't know how. I'm completely at a loss." This was hard to admit, and the helplessness I felt gnawed at my insides. Silently I prayed, "Lord, if he can do anything—Lord, help him!"

I turned from my car, tried to pull my thoughts together, and walked into the meeting house. As we began to sing the from-the-soul Polish hymns I had grown to love, my spirits lifted. Then above the singing I heard a strange noise: tap . . . tap . . . tap . . . tap . . . tap. I couldn't imagine what my young friend was doing! I wondered, "Is he going to do something by *tapping*?" As we sang for the next twenty minutes, the tapping continued.

Shortly after we finished singing, the tapping stopped. When the young man walked in and sat down several minutes later, I was dumbfounded! Could he have already repaired the car? I grew more and more restless as the service continued. I had to force myself to concentrate as I preached. At last we sang the final hymn. I gave the benediction and made my way toward the door. When I walked outside and saw the mechanic standing by my car, my curiosity was piqued. "Well, were you able to repair it?" I blurted.

He grinned at me. "Yes!"

I raised my eyebrows in amazement. "How?"

We looked under the front of my car. "Well, I took a hammer and a punch and just began tapping the two edges together; your crankcase is aluminum, so it has a little flexibility. I simply tapped until the two edges of the crack met; then I turned under the edge of the seam to seal it. Afterwards, I went to a farmer nearby who had some tractor oil, enough to fill your crankcase, and now it's just dripping one drop every so many seconds—but it's okay, you can travel. When you return to Przemysl tomorrow, stop by my shop and I'll do the last touch on it. Then it won't drip at all."

I was overwhelmed to think that God had provided that young mechanic with such an ingenious idea! To me, this was truly miraculous. I did go to his shop the next day and he completely sealed my crankcase. It never leaked again. In fact, two years later I sold that car with this original repair job still holding! What a poignant reminder that the Lord is faithful. Even when we are completely at a loss to know what to do, He will supply exactly what we need.

For three years our nonfunctional printing press gathered dust as I continued with our other French projects. But I had not forgotten about printing and was ready to try again at the first opportunity.

"Brother, is there anything special that you need? I'm afraid to take all this money into the Soviet Union." One of our SGA workers from Australia, a middle-aged woman with graying hair, looked at me expectantly. She had stopped in Billy-Montigny for a few days in 1977 to get over her jet lag before traveling East.

Was there anything I needed? I didn't have to think before answering: "We need an offset press to help us with publicity for our mobile chapel, our church, and for evangelism."

She nodded. "I'll pray about it."

A few days later she approached me. "The Lord has laid it upon my heart to give you some of the money for your press." And she presented me with a $1,200 gift.

I decided to go to Lille, the nearest large city, and price offset presses. I thought we could get a portable one for about three or four thousand dollars, but I was in for a shock. The smallest offset press in the store, a portable model, cost nine thousand dollars. I couldn't believe it.

Next to this small press was an A. B. Dick 250. The salesman spotted me looking at it. "You know, with this machine you could even print books."

Books? Something clicked. Books! Think of what we could do for Eastern Europe if we could print books—Bibles, New Testaments, study guides, Sunday-school booklets, theological books, books for children—the possibilities were endless. The flyers and posters for our mobile chapel could be printed in no time, and then we could print badly needed books for Eastern Europe. This would be tremendous! I turned to the salesman. "What's the price?"

"Ten thousand—just a thousand dollars more than that little portable model."

A thousand dollars' difference didn't seem like too much for the added ability to print books! But ten thousand dollars? I didn't have it. The gentleman sensed my problem and assured me that the price was a steal. "In a few more weeks our prices are going up. Inflation, you know." He smiled sadly. "This press will go up three to five percent. If you can order now, you'll save yourself a lot of money."

Three to five percent would be several hundred dollars more. Maybe my church would help me; maybe other churches would be interested in joining us. I decided to lay the problem before my own congregation first and then try the others.

"You should be more involved in the pastoral work!" A heavyset man in our church had risen to speak and everyone was staring at him. He spoke French with a thick Polish accent, shaking his fist in the air for emphasis. "We don't see you enough as it is. If you buy this printing machine, we won't see you at all. No, I'm not willing to help you buy it." He sat down abruptly and glared at me.

I felt as though someone had thrown a bucket of cold water on me. I had just presented my idea for a printing press. I had explained our need to print material for the mobile chapel and also said that we would be able to print books for our brothers and sisters behind the Iron Curtain. Never had I dreamed that anyone in my congregation would react in such a negative way to such a great opportunity. I wondered how many others silently echoed this man's attitude. Although I was hurt, I wasn't going to beg them to help me. "Okay," I replied, masking my disappointment, "the Lord will provide elsewhere."

A short time later, I presented my idea at a meeting of about thirty pastors from our area. I emphasized that with this printing press we could even print books. "Will you help me in this venture?" I asked.

One of the pastors, a man involved in selling books, knew something about printing. He responded, "Brother Kapitaniuk, I will not encourage you because printing books isn't easy."

I was stunned. Even pastors were not willing to support me. I expected everyone, especially pastors, to share my excitement about printing. Why couldn't I make anyone understand the importance of an undertaking like this? I still believed that the Lord would enable me to get that press if it was what He wanted. So again I didn't force the issue. I scanned the pastors' faces and said, "Certainly the Lord is going to provide somewhere."

Within a few days, an elderly couple from my church, both in their eighties, came to me privately. "We'd like to give you this," they said, and presented me with two thousand dollars from their savings. I was touched to think that these people had caught my vision and were willing to give so sacrificially. Soon others also came to my home and presented me with gifts toward the press. Surely this was an indication that the Lord was with me!

I returned to Lille and made a down payment on the A. B. Dick, believing that the Lord would provide the rest of the money. At last my sons and I could begin printing promotional literature for our mobile chapel—or so I thought. Little did I know that our new press would first be churning out books for Eastern Europe.

"You know, Bill, we have an offer from a Hungarian mission to print twenty thousand Hungarian books for twenty-two thousand dollars." A robust young SGA worker faced me. I had worked with him before when he helped deliver literature to Eastern Europe one summer. Now he was living in Europe and coordinating literature projects for the mission.

As he spoke, I made some quick calculations: a few thousand dollars for paper, a couple thousand for ink. I could offer to do the job for twenty thousand dollars and still clear about five thousand to pay off the remainder owed on my A. B. Dick. "Brother," I interjected, "I'm willing to print that book for only twenty thousand."

He smiled. "If you can do the project at that price, it's yours."

I could barely contain my excitement. Books! We were going to print books for Eastern Europe! And on our own press! At this point, of course, I could only see the final product. I had no idea what lay in store along the way.

The press churned and clacked and thudded to its own rhythm as I looked with growing apprehension around our newly constructed garage. We were well into our Hungarian book project, and evidence of this fact surrounded me. The press itself occupied a sizable area. Huge packages of paper, still in their brown wrappings, were stacked in a corner. Our small trimmer stood inconspicuously off to one side. Make-shift tables overflowed with partially collated book sections. One of my sons was busy at the binding machine, gluing previously collated pages together. Towers of already-printed but not collated sheets of paper covered every available space between the machines and tables. Peter Chartschlaa, a printer's son who had come from America to help us, grunted occasional directions.

To anyone else the scene would have seemed a mass of confusion, but to me, who had seen how far we had come from our original frantic and unprofessional efforts, the situation was blissfully organized—organized but struggling.

It had not taken long for me to realize why my pastor friend had not been enthusiastic about my purchasing a printing press. In my impulsive desire to print books for Eastern Europe, I had overlooked one detail: I had never printed books before. My naiveté had blinded me to everyday realities. I was now up to my ears in a project that I didn't have the proper machinery, know-how, or manpower to produce effectively.

Perhaps our A. B. Dick *could* print books—if they were small—but our Hungarian manuscript was 347 pages long. Our press could handle only eight of those pages on each sheet of paper, four pages on each side. In addition, the press could print only one side at a time, so each sheet had to be run through the press twice.

And a printing press, I soon learned, did not spit out finished books. The printed pages had to be cut and collated. A folding machine would have greatly speeded our production at this point; once printed, the sheets could have been folded and collated. Without a folder, the printed sheets each had to be cut into pages, and each page collated separately—all 347 pages! Once collated, the pages had to be glued. The process seemed never-ending.

I found out the hard way that there is no such thing as a "simple" printing operation. To produce the Hungarian book for which we had contracted, our minimal needs (besides the press) were for a trimmer, a collator, and a binding machine. Such machines were not cheap, but since we couldn't do without them, I had purchased each one as the need arose.

Now I picked up one of the completed books and thumbed through it. The book was a compilation of allegories and pen-and-ink drawings created by Dr. E. J. Pace some sixty years before. I had heard that many years ago pastors in Hungary got hold of this book and enjoyed Pace's articles so much that they had the book translated into Hungarian. They also had some of the sketches redrawn to better fit their situation and somehow had the Hungarian version of the book printed. But the book had long been out of print, and my Hungarian brothers could give me only a tattered copy. They did, however, provide us with negatives, each of which we had to reduce by $\frac{1}{4}''$ (due to the size of paper we wanted to use).

Instead of the twenty thousand copies we had hoped to have for our Hungarian friends, we produced only ten thousand before deciding that we simply couldn't finish the project. Tired and frustrated, we realized that we had taken on too big a job for our small press. We had struggled along printing four pages at a time, we had separately collated 1,735,000 pages; we had coped without a folding machine. We had exhausted our resources and couldn't print the remaining half of the order. (Even though the order wasn't completed and the intended profit made, the A. B. Dick was paid off.)

But I wasn't totally disheartened. And we *had* printed ten thousand Pace books against incredible odds. Later, some months after we had struggled so hard to produce them, I was to hear a story of how the Lord had used one. . . .

A copy of the Pace book had found its way into the home of a Hungarian woman. She was a strong believer, but her husband was an atheist. For many months she had prayed for him and spoken to him about the Lord. She had encouraged him to read the Bible, but he had no interest in it.

One day she had left the Pace book lying on a table when she went out to do some errands. The book caught her husband's attention as he walked through the room, and he started leafing through it. The pictures interested him. He began to read and was captivated by the simple yet profound stories and illustrations. Before he knew it, he had read the whole book.

"That book had a terrific impact on my husband," his wife later declared gratefully. "His whole outlook changed when he read it."

That woman's story was no isolated case. In fact, the Hungarian Pace book was so well received and the demand so great that we reprinted it again when we acquired a larger, more efficient press. In fact, it was the first book we printed on that new press—but that was not till years later.

Now, as I looked at the finished books produced by our A. B. Dick, I realized that we would need to take drastic measures if we wanted to continue printing. Sure, we were struggling, but something about the process had crept under my skin; it thoroughly intrigued me. Besides, we were too involved to give it up now! The search for a bigger press, I knew even then, would be only the first step in expanding our operation.

I looked around the room at the figures assembled, each a member of SGA's field council, and asked, "Why should we give all God's money into the hands of the rich commercial printers, when we can use that money to print our books and make our own shop and do whatever we want?" For months our small print shop had been limping along with a rotoprint press that had replaced our A. B. Dick. Although it could print twice as many pages, the process was still slow and the quality poor. Would I be able to make the field council understand? The looks that greeted me were reserved and calculating. Here's where we would plan our strategy for the next several months. Was my dream of a large-scale printing operation to be back-burnered again?

One of the members cleared his throat and began to speak. "Bill, we have documented proof of several Christian printers who went bankrupt—in Africa, Korea, South America. . . ."

I sighed as the voice droned on. So many times I had heard this argument: Why should we run the risk of printing when so many before us had failed? I tried to appear calm, but my frustration increased. Why were we so quick to see the risk and so slow to see the opportunity? The more I traveled into Eastern Europe, the more I realized that the literature we delivered barely scratched the surface of the great need. Lately I had begun to ask myself, "After twenty-eight years of not beginning to meet the spiritual need of the people, how, with the few remaining years that I have, can I get the job finished?" The more I thought, the more it seemed to me that mass production of literature was the way to go. Gospels, New Testaments, Bibles, Christian books—with thousands of these we could reach masses of people that we would otherwise never reach.

I looked my co-worker straight in the eye as he concluded his argument. "Well," I said, "it seems to me that commercial printers can get the job done without going bankrupt. Why can't we?"

There was a pause. A different voice broke the silence. "But why not print the books in America? It's cheaper."

I had done a little homework, too, and I smiled. "It's one thing to print, but then you have to transport. You have to pack it in America, transport it to a shipping port, ship it, pay for the shipping, and then go through customs here in Europe. Then you have to figure out a way to deliver it to its destination." I stopped for breath and went on: "The price of paper doesn't vary much, and you still have to pay for the paper, whether you print in America or in France. At the present time it's cheaper to buy paper in Europe than in America. And then there's the cost of labor; it's much higher in America than in France. Besides, we're operating as a mission; we keep our labor costs to a minimum. I feel that we could produce books at a much cheaper price than a commercial printer."

"Yes, but Bill—."

The minutes passed as we discussed the pros and cons of expanding our French printing operation. The arguments on both sides were convincing, but not as convincing as the bottom line: Where would we get the money? What I was proposing would cost a great deal, and we couldn't begin expanding until we had assurance that the Lord was providing the necessary funds.

In two years we had raised only a fraction of what we needed to move to a higher level of printing, so the general consensus was to postpone any expansion for the time being. My heart sank. We had such a unique opportunity before us, and I hated to let it slip through our fingers for yet another year. I turned to the council members and asked, "We do have the money that's been raised. What are we going to do with it? Can I use it?"

"Of course. Go ahead and buy the stitcher and collator you need for your present operation."

As the council adjourned I thanked the members for allowing me to purchase two new machines. But I left with a heavy heart.

I felt so very alone. Why did I keep trying to get this printing operation moving, anyway? Our early attempts certainly hadn't met with much success. And often I received criticism and disapproval for my efforts; it was like beating my head against a brick wall. Then, unexpectedly, I remembered someone whom everyone had criticized. Jesus alone was satisfied with what she had done. My mind flashed back to the scene where I had last shared that message with others. . . .

" 'And truly I say to you, wherever the gospel is preached in the whole world, that also which this woman has done shall be spoken of in memory of her' " (Mark 14:9). I looked up and surveyed the sea of faces before me. I was in Poland on a trip I had made before my travel had been restricted, gearing up to deliver a sermon on what I considered one of the Bible's most challenging passages.

I hadn't always thought so; it had taken years for the meaning to sink in. The passage had deeply disturbed me when I first came upon it. Preaching the gospel made sense, but it seemed irrelevant to preach about *Mary* in the whole world (John's Gospel [12:1–3] indicates that Lazarus' sister, Mary, is the woman.). I couldn't see the connection. How could one possibly compare Mary's act with the gospel? Yet there it was in black and white, Jesus instructing His followers to speak about Mary wherever the gospel was preached. Only after months, even years, of studying and meditating did the light begin to dawn on me.

"Now, I ask you, what is the gospel?" I said as I looked into those dear Polish faces. "Let's look at Paul's first epistle to the Corinthians, where it's very clearly defined. 'Now I make known to you, brethren, the gospel which I preached to you, which also you received, in which also you stand, by which also you are saved . . .' (1 Cor. 15:1–2a). The gospel, then, is something tremendous because through it we are saved. But what *is* it?

I answered from Scripture: " 'For I delivered to you as of first importance what I also received, that Christ died for our sins according to the Scriptures, and that He was buried, and that He was raised on the third day according to the Scriptures . . .' (1 Cor. 15:3–4). This is the gospel in a nutshell: Christ died, Christ was buried, Christ was raised again. Christ died for my sins; He took my chastisement and my suffering upon Himself so that I could have forgiveness. He tasted death for me so I wouldn't have to taste its bitterness. And then He was raised again, so there is resurrection, there is hope, there is eternal life. This is the gospel.

"In the second letter Paul wrote to the Corinthians, he focuses on another aspect of the gospel: 'For you know the grace of our Lord Jesus Christ, that though He was rich, yet for our sake He became poor, that you through His poverty might become rich' (2 Cor. 8:9). The gospel is also that Jesus Christ, the King of kings and Lord of lords, became poor that you and I might become rich. When Jesus was speaking of this sacrifice, He took bread, broke it and said, 'This is My body which is given for you; do this in remembrance of Me.' And then He took the cup and He said, 'This cup which is poured out for you is the new covenant in my blood' (Luke 22:19–20). So, here's what I now see as the gospel: Jesus Christ, who was rich, became poor. Jesus Christ broke His body, poured out His soul, for us."

The congregation was hanging on my every word, eager to see the relationship between this well-known gospel message and Mary of Bethany. I continued: "As I was thinking about Mary's act, I began to see the connection Jesus had made between it and preaching the gospel to the end of the earth. At one time, Mary was very rich, because in her home she possessed an alabaster vial of very expensive ointment. But then, one day, she became suddenly poor because she broke that vial and poured its entire contents on Jesus. Her great wealth was lost in a few short minutes.

"What Mary did was not what we would do. For example, when a woman has a bottle of expensive French perfume, what does she do? She opens up that bottle, puts a few drops on her finger and rubs only a little here and a little there, because it's very expensive. If she paid forty or fifty dollars for a tiny bottle of perfume she doesn't just pour it out! But what did Mary do? She *broke,* not opened, the alabaster vial. And because she broke it, she couldn't save any of the contents; she completely emptied the vial with one use.

"That's exactly what Jesus did with His life. His body was broken, and His life completely poured out. The prophet Isaiah spoke of that act: 'As a result of the anguish of His soul, he will see it and be satisifed. . . . Therefore, I will allot Him a portion with the great, and He will divide His booty with the strong; because He poured out

Himself to death . . .' (Isa. 53:11–12a). Jesus broke the bread and told His disciples, 'This is my body, given for you'; Mary broke the alabaster box. Jesus poured out His life; Mary poured out all of the ointment on Jesus. So, in a sense, Mary's act was a miniature gospel act; she actually illustrated what Jesus did.

"I believe that is why Jesus told His disciples to speak of what Mary did wherever they preached the gospel, because if we understand the gospel, we should react as Mary did—we should be willing to sacrifice our most precious possession. Of course, Mary's precious possession was partly symbolic, because the most precious thing that you and I possess is not ointment, it's not money, it's not family, it's not a home. The most precious thing that anyone can possess is *life*! Even Satan knew that when he said to God about Job, 'Skin for skin! Yes, all that a man has he will give for his life' (Job 2:4b). When a person is dying, he is willing to give anything if he can prolong his life even a few extra days. The most important thing, our most precious possession, is our life.

"Jesus gave that precious possession to redeem us. He gave His life, His entire life, that we might know life. He poured out His soul unto death. He gave everything—body, soul, and spirit—as a sacrifice for us because He loved us. His was not a partial giving, but a giving in entirety. Perhaps that's why He commanded us to look at what Mary did. Her gift wasn't half-hearted, nor was it partial. She didn't just dab a few drops of ointment here and there; she gave it all.

"Very often as Christians we are tempted to do as those ladies with the expensive French perfume; we dab a little here and a little there. We give a few drops of our time to the Lord: a few minutes in the morning, a few minutes at night, an hour or so on Sunday. 'Lord,' we say, 'this is enough. I've got no time. The rest is for me.'

"This was not Mary's attitude. By that one loving act, she exemplified what our attitude should be if we truly understand our Lord's sacrifice for us: a willingness to give ourselves totally to Him. Not just a few minutes here and there but *all* our time, *all* our life. The question we need to ask is not, 'Lord, how much am I supposed to give?' but rather, 'Lord, how much am I supposed to keep for myself?' This is the true gospel that Mary exemplified in her sacrificial act."

Nods and murmurs of assent rippled through the congregation, and I smiled as I saw understanding spread across the faces before me. I thanked the Lord and went on: "We read in John's Gospel that 'the house was filled with the fragrance of the ointment' (John 12:3b). For the first time that perfume was useful. Flowers can at least be partially enjoyed by looking at them, but where's the enjoyment in looking at a bottle of perfume? The only way you can enjoy perfume is by smelling it!

"As Christians we either give off a pleasant aroma or a disagreeable stink. We all know people—Christians—whom nobody wants to be around. Their lives, their conduct, their manner of speaking, and their attitude are such that we avoid them. This is not as it should be! We Christians should have a sweet aroma, the perfume of Christ's loving goodness, patience, and kindness. But this only happens when we are broken, when we completely give ourselves to Jesus Christ. As long as we love ourselves and live only for ourselves, we cannot be that perfume of Christ. But when we are broken like Mary's alabaster box, when we give our lives as a 'living sacrifice' to Jesus, then His fragrance will flow from our lives, filling up our houses. We will give off sweet perfumes that our families, our neighbors, and our co-workers will enjoy.

"This is what I see in Mary's sacrifice. She could have been selfish and kept that perfume for herself. But she didn't; she broke the vial and gave all the perfume to Jesus. It's only when our lives are broken that we begin to give off that sweet perfume. If we aren't broken, if we try to keep our lives contained for our own selfish pleasures and ambitions, no one will profit from them. People, in fact, will be repelled by us."

The congregation looked very solemn. I knew that what I was saying was not easy to practice in everyday life, especially in a country like Poland. But to me, the best part of this little allegory was yet to come, so I smiled when I continued: "Now, you'll recall that Mary wasn't encouraged for her action; in fact, she met with bitterness and resentment. The disciples began to grumble among themselves, 'For what purpose has this perfume been wasted? For this perfume might have been sold for over three hundred denarii, and the money given to the poor' (Mark 14:4–5). Then they turned to Mary and began scolding her!

"Now why were the disciples so bitter? I think they were infected by Judas. We know from the Gospel of John that Judas, as treasurer, used to pilfer money from the money box (John 12:6). He selfishly wanted that perfume so that he could sell it and fatten his wallet on the proceeds. No doubt his attitude had affected several other disciples. Unfortunately, this is what often happens in a church; one person poisons the whole atmosphere and everybody begins to sing his song. The disciples must have realized the profit that could have been made by selling that perfume! When Mary broke that vial, there was nothing left for her, nothing left for them. From a human point of view, she'd wasted something very precious.

"But the good thing about it was what the Lord said. And that we should never forget. 'Let her alone; why do you bother her? She has done a good deed to Me' (Mark 14:6). That simple statement has been perhaps the greatest source of encouragement in my life. Jesus was satisfied with what Mary did. One thing I've learned that keeps me going when things are rough, regardless of what other people think and say about me, is this: The only thing that really matters is, 'What does the Lord think and say about me?' If He can say to me at the end of my life, 'Bill, I'm pleased with your life; well done, thou good and faithful servant,' this is what really counts for me."

I remembered that the congregation had been silent then, mulling over my final thoughts. And as I thought about the field council meeting that had so recently distressed me, I realized that I, too, needed the reminder that the most important thing in life is what the Lord thinks about me. Just as Mary's commitment went beyond trying to please anyone except her Lord, so I, too, needed to remember that my ultimate commitment was to Jesus Christ, and I had to do what I felt He wanted me to do, regardless of what others thought. For some reason He had shown me the great need in Eastern Europe for the printed page. And, beyond reason, I felt compelled to try to meet that need. Sure, I would probably make mistakes—I had already made several—but I remembered that someone once said that the only one who doesn't make mistakes is the one who doesn't do anything. Ultimately, God was the One to whom I would have to give an account. And I believed with all my heart that He wanted me to establish a large-scale printing ministry for Eastern Europe.

Meanwhile, the heart of Poland churned in the wake of a series of cataclysmic events. Her inner turmoil culminated in the advent of what would come to be known as the Solidarity Crisis. The world looked on with mounting concern as Solidarity dominated news headlines.

Little did I know it then, but these events would completely change my involvement in Poland. In 1975, as they were still fermenting, my travel restrictions to Poland were lifted.

10

Holy Cheese, Motor Oil, and Bridge Builders

We'll have to change the fuel filter." The burly French truck driver looked at me with resignation as he opened the cab door of the semi-trailer and stepped out into the early sub-zero morning. It was the winter of 1981, and we were on an East German freeway, headed for the Polish border.

On December 13, radio receivers had crackled with the news that a "state of war" had been declared in Poland. SGA co-workers from England had been inadvertently caught in the crisis and confirmed what we had been hearing about the desperate need for food, clothing, and medicines. Now I was en route to Poland in a thirty-eight-ton semi-trailer truck filled with relief goods.

We had left a bitterly cold France and arrived in East Germany at one in the morning. Exhausted from some difficulties that we had encountered already, we stopped for a brief

149

rest. After an hour's nap, we started the engine and moved onto the freeway, only to have our truck stall. The extreme cold was causing problems for us, even as extremes in the economic and political climates of Poland had been causing problems within her borders for several years. . . .

Much had transpired in my beloved Poland since my travel ban had taken effect in 1970. By the latter part of that year, Gomulka's efforts at stabilizing the economy had failed so badly that on December 13, the government was forced to impose a series of price increases. These increases were rather clumsily disguised; prices for luxury items such as tape-recorders, TV sets, and car radios were lowered, while prices for necessities like food and clothing increased.

This new tactic, as well as its poor timing, just twelve days before Christmas, generated discontent and unrest throughout the country. Infuriated workers along the Baltic coast showed their disfavor by launching a protest strike. On December 16, the government violently intervened, suppressing the strike by tank and helicopter attacks. No one knows how many people were killed or injured. Official figures listed 45 dead and 1,165 wounded, but unofficial estimates were much higher. This event resulted in the "resignation" of Gomulka but, more seriously, it was a wound that began to fester in the hearts of Poland's people.

In 1975 I was permitted to travel into Poland once again. At one point during my five-year wait, my Christian friends in Poland had written, "You'd better come and visit us. We need thirty tons of paper." I wrote back: "Okay; get me a visa to enter your country and I'll provide you with the paper." I was frustrated by my travel restrictions and was trying every conceivable channel to be allowed to visit Poland. Later I learned that the Christians had indeed visited the government authorities and pled with them to let me in. Eventually the authorities relented, and from 1975 to the present I have made several trips into Poland to continue my varied outreaches.

By 1976, the Polish debt to the West had risen to $11 billion—a shocking increase from the $2.5 billion of only three years earlier. A chief Polish economist sent a letter to Gierek, the new first secretary of the Polish Communist Party, warning of the very real possibility of economic disaster. In order to boost the faltering economy, Gierek announced a 60 percent increase in food prices. Once again, sit-down strikes swept the country; prices were rolled back and the strikes fizzled out.

Poland's economic problems had become so serious by mid-1980 that her debt to the West was more than $20 billion. On July 1, a government decree raised most meat prices nearly 100 percent, supposedly because of a scarcity of supply. However, many Poles believed that their meat was being shipped to Moscow to feed those attending the Moscow Summer Olympics and were understandably upset. (Later I actually saw a semi-trailer truck loaded with meat leaving Poland.) Localized strikes broke out all over the country. The government pacified some workers by offering slight pay increases, but many workers were not satisfied—most notably those in Gdansk. By August 8, more than 150 factories were on strike.

Tension mounted as workers' demands were debated and nego-tiated. Finally, on August 31, the government and the Gdansk strikers signed an agreement, including improved health and working conditions; the sanctioning of free, independent trade unions with the right to strike; Saturdays off; and Sunday masses to be broad-cast over the radio. On September 15, the government declared that these accords were applicable to the entire country.

On September 22, delegates from thirty-six regional independent unions made history in Gdańsk by uniting under the name "Solidar-ity." By the end of 1980, with debts to the West soaring at $23 billion, the Polish government pointed to scarcities in food and other supplies in pleading for an end to labor unrest.

But the labor unrest had just begun. Throughout 1981, Solidarity dominated the headlines with sporadic strikes and demands. The authorities again resorted to violence, which further incensed work-ers and increased the tension. By the end of April, Poland's debt to the West exceeded $25 billion. Meat rationing had begun on April 1; by May 1, rationing was extended to a variety of products. I think the Polish government was, in part, trying to put pressure on Solidarity by rationing food and increasing prices. It tried to show that the situation was not going to get better, but worse, as long as Solidarity made demands. But tensions, strikes, food prices, and rationing continued to mount until December 13, when General Jaruzelski declared Poland to be in "a state of war." Such was the turmoil we headed toward with our relief supplies. . . .

I shivered as I tried to shine the flashlight on our fuel filter. The temperature had dropped to twenty degrees below zero, and I could think of half a dozen places I would rather be than stalled along an East German highway in the wee hours of the morning. A biting wind penetrated my heavy coat, hat, and mittens as though they were made of cotton gauze. In silent amazement I watched the truck driver change our fuel filter with his bare hands. We were half-frozen as we climbed back into the cab. But our engine still wouldn't start.

The driver turned to me. "I'll bet our fuel is frozen." He reached for an old rag, some oil, and matches, and once more we climbed from the cab into the cold.

He saturated the rag with oil, set it on fire and held it under our fuel tank. Half an hour later, the fuel was warmed sufficiently so that we could start the truck. But the driver found that our real problem was a burnt-out fuse in the fuel tank's heating apparatus, and if we didn't remedy that, our fuel would soon freeze again. After he short-circuited a breaker and got our heating apparatus functioning, we resumed our travel and soon arrived at the Polish border.

Our weather-related problems were soon forgotten as we entered the border complex where the tension enveloped us like a fog. Only during the Mideast crisis had I seen the border bristling with so many customs officials, militia, and guard dogs. There must have been twice as many personnel as usual, all striving for cool professionalism. And the bitter cold aggravated the situation.

After our passport inspection and other preliminaries, officials told us to remove the tarpaulin from one side of our truck. The tarp was forty-five feet long, and we didn't relish standing in the freezing cold, but we had to comply. Then five men arbitrarily selected boxes to check.

"Open that one!" a gruff voice demanded.

We hauled a huge box off the truck and opened it for a customs officer and militia man to inspect. This in itself was a break from usual procedure, as only one person would normally inspect each box. This process was repeated about twenty times, from one end of the truck to the other. At last they were satisfied that all we carried was food, clothing, and medicine. "Pack up and you can go!" an official finally barked.

If we had thought the atmosphere on the border was tense, the full gravity of the situation became all too clear as we entered Poland. Military people were everywhere. There was a checkpoint every several kilometers where army tanks stood at the crossroads and checked us through. In addition, military officials stopped us at random and examined our passports, so, besides the dozens of periodic checkpoints, we quickly became accustomed to arbitrary checks as we traveled. All this to deliver much-needed relief goods!

By the time we reached the southeastern town of Brzeg, the tension had begun to wear on me. This was not the Poland I remembered. What must it be like for those who had to live in this kind of atmosphere day after day?

Dusk was settling as we turned down a narrow, poorly paved road. The snow squeaked as our tires crunched it. Hardly a soul ventured out into the freezing cold, and the streets were eerily empty. The only signs of life were curls of smoke rising from the chimneys of the buildings we passed. Suddenly I spotted a familiar house and pointed it out to the driver. He parked our semi and I hopped down from the cab. I knocked on the door and stood shivering, beating my arms against myself to stay warm. The door opened a crack and a pair of dark eyes peeped out at me from under a set of bushy eyebrows.

"It's me! Bill Kapitaniuk!" I cried, the cold cutting through me like a knife. At the mention of my name, the door flew open and strong arms reached out and pulled me into the warmth.

The next few moments were a blur of delighted squeals, kisses, and bear hugs as dear Christian friends, a family I knew well, surrounded me. Someone peeled off my coat, hat, and mittens, led me to the kitchen and ordered me to sit. The next thing I knew, a cup of steaming tea was thrust into my hands and everyone tried to speak at once in the animated Polish fashion I had grown to love so well.

As I sat in the midst of this jumble, the husband and father of the family approached me. "You know, we had a feeling you might be coming today," he said. I raised my eyebrows in surprise. I hadn't told anyone I was coming; how could he have expected me?

He smiled at my expression. "Last night I had a dream that you were coming, so at breakfast this morning I told the family. We wondered what this meant. Would you really come? All day long, every time we heard a car drive past or a dog bark, we ran to the window; we thought it was you!"

I didn't know what to say. How humbling to think that the Lord had let this dear family know I would be coming! And, as yet, they had no idea of the cargo we carried. I smiled as I imagined what their reaction would be. I didn't have to speculate long. As the driver and I unloaded box after box of food, medicine, and clothes, we couldn't help but notice my Polish friends. Their eyes opened wide, their mouths dropped, and they were so overwhelmed that they could barely speak.

After many months of high prices, the recent rationing, and the seemingly endless days of having to do without, our simple gifts of sugar, butter, and canned meat were priceless treasures. It was heartwarming to see their gratitude. And, as we learned later, once we had the supplies in the hands of church leaders, each church formed committees and shared according to the need of every family in that church.

Thus began our series of trips into Poland with relief goods. Each was different, touched with its own shade of miracle.

"Look. We have nothing left for the children." The director of the Polish orphanage had opened his cold-storage room.

The situation was the same throughout Poland—many centers were down to their last crumb. I had never seen such hard times in Poland. The early 1980s were years of hardship for everyone, including government officials and institutions. The scarcity of food and medicine was shocking.

Generous Christians from around the world had rallied to Poland's need. Our garage in Billy-Montigny had become a receiving and storage center for goods that poured in from all over Europe. In addition to supplies, financial gifts arrived from France, Great Britain, Austria, North America—even Australia—and I was constantly figuring how to get the best values for this money.

Often the Lord provided in ways I would never have imagined, and as I looked at the orphanage's empty storeroom, I smiled. On this particular trip I had something to help fill it that they wouldn't have dreamed of in a thousand years. I remembered the "coincidence" by which our cargo was obtained. . . .

"Do you have any inexpensive cheese for sale? I'm trying to fill a twenty-five-ton truck with food and other relief supplies for Poland." I had called a cheese factory in France to see if they had any cheese I could buy at a discount.

The voice on the other end of the line sounded surprised. "As a matter of fact, we have some cheese we can't sell on the French market—some mimolette. It didn't turn out like it was supposed to; it has holes inside and, as you know, mimolette is not supposed to have holes." He paused. "We'll sell it at half the price that it cost us to produce it. Normally it costs us twenty-two francs a kilo to produce; we'll sell it to you for ten."

Ten francs a kilo! That was just a little more than a dollar for over two pounds of perfectly good cheese. "How much of this cheese do you have?"

"Seven tons."

I hesitated. The price was terrific, but even so, seven tons of cheese would cost close to seven thousand dollars. Perhaps I could find some other food at a comparable price. "I'll order three tons," I said, and hung up.

Those seven tons of cheese haunted me the rest of the afternoon. The more I thought about it, the more I realized that there was no other good food we could buy for ten francs a kilo. So I called the cheese factory back and told them we'd take the whole seven tons. . . .

"Our truck is burning!" I stared in disbelief as clouds of blue smoke poured out of the truck carrying the remaining five tons of mimolette cheese. Instead of riding in the truck, this time I was traveling through Poland in my car and had to stop because the smoke was so dense. We had already stopped at two or three churches and at the orphanage to unload part of the cheese. But we still carried the bulk of it for our final destination—if we ever made it.

Moments later, when I could see to drive, I passed the truck and the two of us pulled over to the side of the road. I scrambled out of the car and met the truck driver in front of his engine. "What happened?" I asked.

"The turbo cracked. I stopped here because I'm out of oil."

No more oil? As this sank in, I realized that the clouds of dark smoke that had prevented me from driving must have represented thirty liters of oil—all burned up in about ten minutes! And here we were in Poland on a Saturday, during a state of war, out in the country and miles from a garage. We locked the truck's cab and drove my car the nine kilometers to the house where we were supposed to be unloading our remaining supplies. But the pastor wasn't there.

"He's at the church," the pastor's wife, a young, dark-haired woman, told us with a rueful smile. The church was a little distance from their home; two pastors lived in that area and shared the pastoral duties. We had no recourse but to go to the church. We were near the extreme northwestern tip of Poland, and the church was in Świnoujście, on an island just west of us. This meant we had to take a ferry to the island.

As the ferry unloaded, we headed straight for the church. But it was empty. So was the other pastor's home.

Now what? We stopped at the post office to phone the truck driver's garage in France. (In European countries, international public telephones are often located in post offices.) But the post office personnel weren't very helpful. "No," they told us, "it's Saturday; we can't have any communication with the outside world on Saturday while we're in this state of war."

We were close to the East German border at this point, so I said to the truck driver, "Maybe we can phone for help from East Germany." We drove to the border and explained our predicament to the officials. But they shook their heads. "No," one of them remarked, "on Saturday everything is closed. You can't phone from here."

I sighed for the umpteenth time that day. One of the officials suggested we find a garage where we could get a truck to pull our semi. But in that area, no one had a truck large enough to pull our huge American Mack. (Many of the trucks we rented from French agencies were from the States.)

We must have looked forlorn, because the East German officials were doing their best to be helpful. In the course of our conversation, one remarked, "Why don't you go back to the ferry and ask if you can send a Telex via Sweden? From Sweden they could send a Telex to the garage near Paris you're trying to reach."

Something in my mind clicked as he said that. I knew there was a Telex connection from Poland to Sweden. Perhaps we had finally found some help! We hopped in the car, turned it around, and once again took the ferry back to the mainland. Then we sped to the Polish port that received ferries from Sweden. I dashed into the office and asked, "Can we send a Telex from here?"

A man looked at me and said, "The office just closed. It'll be open at seven this evening."

I ran my hand through my hair and stifled a groan. I glanced at the truck driver, who looked as frustrated as I. "Let's go back, then," I said, knowing we could do nothing more but take the ferry back to Świnoujście and try to locate the pastor, as I had no other Christian contacts in this area.

When we arrived, there were at least fifty cars waiting to get on the ferry, and the attendant ushered us to the end of the line. It was three in the afternoon and we hadn't had anything to eat since morning. I threw my hands up in the air. "I give up! It's useless to rush around anymore. Let's go get something to eat."

We left the line and I drove to a parking lot and stopped the car. I glanced out the window before stepping out and my mouth dropped open. There, not four feet from me, was the young pastor for whom we had been searching so diligently!

"Brother Kapitaniuk!" He caught sight of me at almost the same time I saw him. My car door was open and, in his glee, he pulled me out and locked me in a great Polish bear hug.

"What are you doing here?" I asked.

"My car broke down and I've been trying to repair it for the last hour."

I shook my head. "Oh, Lord," I prayed, "You still know where we are! In a town of sixty thousand people, you place me right here with this pastor."

After talking a moment, the pastor turned the key in his ignition and his car started! So the truck driver and I hopped back into our car and followed him to his home, where over a meal we explained our predicament. Also at the table, taking in the story, was the pastor's brother. He had arrived that day for a vacation, having traveled over six hundred miles from a town near the Russian border. When we finished describing the dreadful shape of our turbo, this fellow turned to us and said, "You know, I'm a truck driver—and also a diesel specialist."

A diesel specialist! "Well, what would you suggest? Can you repair such a thing?"

"Sure," he told us.

"But how—where?"

His eyes sparkling, he said, "I can repair it right where it is. All I need is a piece of tin, a pair of tin snips, a hammer, a chisel, and a hacksaw. And, of course, some oil."

Oil. Where would we find oil on a Saturday, with everything closed and the country in a state of war? The first two stations we tried were closed. An attendant was at the third one but said we had to find the manager to get some oil. We located the manager's house and caught him just before he went off fishing. We begged him to open his gas station and sell us some oil. He agreed, and soon we were heading out to our truck in the countryside with thirty liters of oil.

It was already six in the evening when we arrived. The pastor's brother went to work and in no time repaired the truck well enough to travel. The turbo wasn't functioning, so the truck lacked the power it ordinarily would have had, but at least it could be driven.

We drove back to the pastor's house and by eleven o'clock had unloaded the last five tons of cheese, as well as other supplies. I shook hands with my truck driver, who was about to begin the long trek back to France in our "lame duck."

The next day, the pastor and I set out for another church, taking some of the cheese. This church was having a baptismal service with about 150 people attending. As was the custom, after the baptism we gathered for a meal. Many foods were scarce during those hard times, and it was touching to see how thrilled these folks were with the cheese.

The pastor decided to make a speech: "God miraculously provided for us by making holes in that cheese. If that cheese had no holes, it would never have come to us; it would have been too expensive. But the Lord has provided food for this special occasion!" Thus we came to call that cheese "holy cheese"!

I thanked God for the chance to provide for Poland's physical needs, but I longed to once again provide for her spiritual hunger, too. An opportunity came when the SGA office in Wheaton, Illinois, shipped us ten thousand copies of the Polish *Life of Christ* book. We soon began to build a bridge of books to Poland . . . .

"Okay, unload everything!" the Polish official said gruffly from the back of the truck, brandishing a copy of *Life of Christ*.

I stared incredulously. How had he managed to find that book? All our literature was in the front of the trailer, safe from scrutinizing eyes—or so I had thought. As my mind raced over the events of the past few days, I realized what had probably happened. In our scramble to finish loading the truck, someone must have carelessly thrown a box of these books into the back of the trailer with all the clothes, food, and medicines. And somehow, from all the boxes he could have chosen, the customs official had managed to lay his hands on that one box of books in the midst of our other boxes.

This was to have been so different from our other relief trips! Besides our usual supplies, we were carrying seven thousand copies of *Life of Christ* (full-color illustrated Gospels) and six hundred Polish Bibles. I had told the Polish consulate in Lille that I would be delivering books and that my friends in Warsaw were requesting a permit for them. But the people in the consulate had not added books to the long list of relief supplies on our declaration papers. In addition, the permit didn't arrive by the time I needed to leave France, so I had decided to travel to Poland without it.

When we reached the Polish border, the customs man had climbed into our truck and began to search through the boxes. That's when he came upon the *Life of Christ* books. Of course, now he wanted to examine the whole load.

Unload our entire trailer—all twenty-four tons of supplies? I threw my hands up in despair. "How can I unload all this? I can't!"

"We won't allow you into the country unless you unload." His grim face didn't look ready for compromise. Then, under his breath, he asked, "How many books do you have?"

I wasn't sure what to say. The official didn't know for sure that we had more books, but that one box he had discovered had given him a clue. I decided to bide my time. "Oh, a few boxes."

"How many boxes?" The voice was penetrating.

I shifted uncomfortably. "Maybe ninety."

"And how many in a box?"

"Oh, about ninety books to a box." I tried to sound casual.

As I spoke, the official started figuring. He raised his head when he finished calculating and asked me to come into the office with him, where I endured an hour of nonstop questioning. I told him that we also had six hundred Polish Bibles, since—if worse came to worst and we were forced to unload— I wanted to be sure I had told him the whole truth. Finally he shook his head and said, "You'll have to unload everything and show us all those books."

This was unthinkable to me. Twenty-four tons—it would take us forever! As far as I was concerned, it wasn't even an option. So once again I refused. Because of my refusal, we had to stay at the border from seven in the evening until eight the next morning. Three of us—two British colleagues and I—had to sleep in our car in sub-zero weather. In the morning, we didn't even have anything hot to drink. It was a terrible experience.

At 8:00 A.M. the customs official approached me again. "Well, start unloading the truck."

During the night, I had formulated a plan of action. "Excuse me, but let me phone Warsaw first."

He agreed, but it was Saturday (why did all my crises take place on Saturdays?), during the "state of war" when communication via telephone was virtually impossible. I was permitted to go down to the basement of the customs building, where a truck dispatcher was operating a telephone. "Please," I asked, "I need to phone Warsaw. Could you help me?"

A pair of dark eyes regarded me coldly, and two thick fingers flicked some cigarette ashes as the dispatcher shook his head. "It's not possible."

"But I need to get a message—"

"I can't." His voice was indifferent, almost a monotone.

His indifference annoyed me. Cold, tired, and hungry, I didn't feel like dealing with this kind of attitude. "You don't understand, I need to send a message to Warsaw. Please!" I'm sure my voice betrayed my frustration.

"No, *you* don't understand!" He sounded annoyed himself. "This is a state of war; it will take six hours to make contact with Warsaw from the border right now."

"Well, I'll just have to wait. But try, please!" I begged him, pled with him for a long time, but he stubbornly kept refusing. Finally, probably to get me off his back, he agreed to try. I dashed out to the car to pick up my briefcase, and as I returned to that little basement room, the phone rang.

The dispatcher hardly looked up as I entered. He nodded at the phone without changing his expression. "It's for you."

I picked it up eagerly, but the dispatcher had dialed the wrong number. I turned to him in exasperation; frustration was turning to panic. "Please, try once more. This is the number," I said, handing him a slip of paper.

But this time the dispatcher refused to cooperate. The more I begged him, the more adamant he became. "No! You go and do your telephoning somewhere else. I've got no time for you."

What could I do? I was desperate. So I pulled out my wallet and took out a five-dollar bill. I slapped it down on the table. "Here. Place my call."

Without another word he scooped up the money and immediately placed my call. Five minutes later, the phone was ringing in Warsaw, and a familiar voice answered. I had caught my pastor friend just in time; he was on his way out the door when he heard the phone.

"Listen, I'm here at the border," I explained hurriedly. I had no idea how long our connection would last, so I raced along. "We've been here for about fifteen hours, and we have books, food, clothes, and medicines. They want us to unload all twenty-four tons so they can see our books. Could you help us?"

He understood immediately. "Okay. I'll do all that I can." He hung up and I breathed a prayer of thanks. If anything could be done to help us, this man would know what it was.

I went back to the car and we sat waiting for several hours. Finally, around noon, the customs official came over to us. "Okay, we'll seal the truck," he said brusquely, "and you drive directly to Warsaw."

I sighed with relief. "Praise God! That's terrific!"

In a matter of hours, I was embracing the pastor I had spoken with earlier. "What did you do?" I asked him.

"Immediately after you called, I rushed to the government buildings and met with some officials. I explained your predicament; they must have sent a Telex to the border so that the customs officials would release you."

Those were the first *Life of Christ* books that we took into Poland, and they spread like wildfire across the country. Wherever they went, people asked for more. Inside the back cover of each book was SGA's U.S.A. address, so people by the hundreds began to write to America for a copy. Many letters were from children, some from teachers. But all were a result of people having seen a copy of *Life of Christ* somewhere in Poland:

"Please send me the *Life of Christ* book. I am Catholic and want to know more about Jesus Christ."

"I am sick with asthma. When I was in the hospital I read a book, *Life of Christ.* I would really like to have it. Books like that interest me very much."

From a nun in Warsaw: "Please send me as many copies as possible of the *Life of Christ.*"

"Recently my girlfriend brought to school the most wonderful colorful book about Christ. I really want to have a book like that."

"I thank you so much for the books you sent me. I do believe that those who are not united to the Lord will be reached through this literature."

These letters indicated the great spiritual need and increased my desire to provide Christian literature for the people of Poland. I firmly believed, along with the writer of the last letter above, that these books would touch the hearts and lives of those who read them. But I wondered how we could transport large loads of literature to Poland. Strangely, the answer came partially through our involvement in providing relief supplies.

"But, why do you pay?" A frown creased the stocky brow of one of the Polish government ministers. "If you have any medicine to send to our country, put it on a plane; we'll pay for the freight. If you have any food or clothes, call our Polish consulate in Paris and we'll provide you with transportation." He leaned forward and folded his thick hands on his desk. A smile curled the edges of his mouth.

I eyed the official warily from my chair in front of his desk. Free transportation? At this point, we had delivered a couple of semi-trailersful of relief goods to Polish orphanages, hospitals, and churches. I knew we had found favor with Polish officials because of our involvement, but I hadn't expected this type of cooperation!

Polish church leaders had been quick to share the goods we brought them—not only with members of their congregations, but also with their neighbors as well as with government officials. Those simple yet welcome parcels were great bridge builders. Little by little, officials began to trust the evangelical leaders.

As we from abroad became involved with relief efforts, our involvement was always linked with the evangelicals in Poland. Thus we, too, gained favor in the eyes of government officials. I had come to know this particular official early in my travels and visited him in his home nearly every trip.

But repeated trips were becoming expensive; the truck rental alone cost between two and three thousand dollars each time. I knew we could greatly multiply our efforts if we could channel that money into more relief supplies.

By now I felt comfortable enough with this Polish government minister to mention that the truck-rental expenses were hampering our relief efforts. I was thrilled with his generous offer to transport our relief goods free of charge, but was puzzled too. How could the Polish government afford it? My host explained to me that Polish trucks left their country with goods to sell to the West, but Poland was in such debt that the trucks had to return to their country empty. It would be a simple matter for the truck dispatcher in Paris to reroute trucks through Billy-Montigny on their return to Poland. We could then fill them with relief goods. Now, instead of returning empty, the trucks could return full—and with relief provisions for which Poland wouldn't have to pay a penny!

I eyed him thoughtfully. If the Polish government was so gracious as to offer transportation for supplies—and it had become so open to the work of evangelicals in general—a wild thought flew through my mind. Could it be remotely possible? It was a long shot, but maybe, just maybe. . . . I cleared my throat. "Sir, suppose one day I have ten thousand Bibles to bring into your country. Would you provide transportation for *them* free of charge?"

The official thought for a minute, his brows knit together as he stared at his desk. Then he looked up at me and smiled.

"Yes, if you have an authorization permit from our government to import them, we'll deliver them."

As I was driving back to France later, I thought about the request I had made. Where was I going to get ten thousand Polish Bibles? I had no idea, but with an offer like that for transportation, I was sure I'd find them somewhere.

11

"All Things Are Possible . . ."

And were you happy with the decision?" The middle-aged gentleman stirred his tea as he looked at me thoughtfully.

"No, not very," I admitted. "Before anything else we need better quality printing, and with our old offset machine we don't have good quality."

I was visiting a friend in Europe after the SGA field-council meeting in which I had proposed setting up a full-scale printing operation in France. I was far from pleased with the council's lack of enthusiasm and limited vision despite the minor concession I had been granted: a green light to upgrade my present machinery by purchasing a collator and a binder. I was still itching to go into printing on a larger scale, but for the time being—until the Lord provided the funds and the necessary personnel—we had to make do with our slow-moving rotoprint press and its barely adequate output.

"Well, what do you need?" My friend frowned. He had always shown an interest in my work into Poland and had once provided the money for a truckload of paper that enabled the Christians in Poland to print within the country. He had also given funds for our early printing efforts in France.

What did I need? That "need" seemed no longer a possibility; it was a wild dream of expanding our printing operation to produce more literature. My thoughts turned to Eastern Europe and to the scarcity of Christian books that I could help alleviate if only I had the means. Was my dream to remain a dream? Must I pretend to be satisfied with the tiny trickle of books we had managed to produce? Had the Lord shut the door on my desire to see Eastern Europe flooded with Christian literature? As my thoughts tumbled together, an old event stirred in my mind and I smiled. No, I wouldn't give up hope just yet. I remembered how my vision of Operation Launch Pad was first born and that the Lord had shown me then that it was easier to take in *more* literature than *less.* . . .

"John, listen to this!" I was at a mission station in Austria with an SGA colleague and was reading that morning's selection from *Streams in the Desert.*

In mid-1969 we had just completed the trip where we spent the better part of the night at the Hungarian-Romanian border trying to convince officials to allow us into Romania with our literature (see chapter 7). After we were finally permitted to take that lone suitcase of literature with us, we delivered it, picked up the twelve cartons of books we had been forced to leave on the Romanian border, traversed Hungary, and arrived in Austria. We were exhausted, bewildered, and frustrated.

Part of the problem was that we had to decide on what to do with our remaining literature. Since we hadn't anticipated any problems in Romania, we couldn't just return to France saying, "Well, we're sorry, but we spent all this money and used all this gas to deliver one suitcase." We had already told our supporters how convinced we were that God wanted us to deliver literature into Eastern Europe.

We had visas for one more country: Czechoslovakia, one of the most difficult to penetrate with Christian literature. Should we try to go and take literature with us? And, if so, how *much* literature? A little? A lot? We prayed but had no clear answer. As we puzzled over a solution, we asked our friends at the Austrian mission to pray with us.

The next morning, March 28, I picked up *Streams in the Desert,* as was my habit, and was amazed at the timeliness of the words before me. "John," I blurted, "listen to this: 'One of the special marks of the Holy Ghost in the Apostolic church was the spirit of boldness. One of the most essential qualities of the faith that is to attempt great things for God, and expect great things from God, is holy audacity. Where we are dealing with a supernatural Being, and taking from Him things that are humanly impossible, it is easier to take much than little . . . like wise seamen in the life of faith, let us launch out into the deep, and find that all things are possible with God . . . let us today attempt great things for God; take His faith and believe for them and His strength to accomplish them.'"

John and I looked at each other without speaking. One phrase had burned itself into my brain: "It is easier to take much than little." "Well," I said quietly to John, "here's our answer." We offered a prayer of thanks and then added, "Okay, Lord; if it's easier to take in much than little, that's exactly what we're going to do."

We went out to the car and pulled out the twelve cartons of books. We broke the Romanian seals on each carton and reloaded our car with all the books we had, stuffing some into our suitcases, and left Austria for Czechoslovakia.

But our "holy audacity" began to wane as we approached the border; the situation was far worse than we had imagined. Cars ahead of us were literally taken apart before our eyes—even entire seats were pulled out of their places. Were we really doing what God wanted us to do? In desperation I cried out, "Lord! We can't allow our car to be taken apart! We're loaded with literature!" My heart was racing and my palms were sweaty. We inched closer and closer to the border compound, praying fervently and entrusting our situation to God. The matter was out of our hands now; there was simply nothing we could do except trust God.

When we arrived at the border, I stepped out of the car with our passports and entered the visa office. A new monkey wrench was tossed into the gears: the officials discovered that my visa was not in order. They kept asking me why I hadn't filled out the form properly, but it was not *my* mistake. When I had purchased the visa, officials at the Czech embassy had filled out the form! Regardless of whose mistake it was, it delayed us many precious minutes at the border. Finally the problem was corrected, our passports were returned, and I left the building. As I approached our car, I noticed that the customs man waiting there was extremely jittery. He had been waiting a long time for those passports so he could check our car.

I handed him the passports; he leafed through them and then looked up at me. "Okay. Open up the back door."

"Oh, Lord!" I cried silently. "Not the *back* door!" Our station wagon was crammed full, and between the front seat and the back were over seven hundred Bibles and Christian books. Of all the places this official could choose to look! But I complied, praying silently as my heart pounded.

The customs man had barely reached into the car when suddenly, just as he slid his hands under the blankets and pillows covering our books, a jeep drove past. As if by a prearranged signal, when the official caught sight of the jeep, he immediately backed away from our car. "Okay, good; you may go."

Was I hearing correctly? I closed the back door, walked in a daze around the car, and slid into the driver's seat. John turned his wide eyes on me. "Are we finished?" he whispered hoarsely.

"Yes," I assured him.

The tension of the last several days had taken its toll on both of us, and now John broke down and began to weep. I took his arm and shook him. "John, it's okay; the official said we're clear," I whispered.

It was only as we drove away that we realized what had happened. By the time the mistake in my visa had been corrected, it was already 12:00 noon, time for the change of shift. The jeep that had driven past us was the dinner jeep, and our official's sudden change of heart was in reality a simple response to his growling stomach. He was more interested in his lunch than in our vehicle!

Were it not for the delay that my visa caused, our literature would most certainly have been discovered. The Lord had once more provided exactly what was needed, His precise timing perfect to the final second. At one point all had appeared utterly hopeless; then, in an instant, we were pulled from our dilemma to a place of safety. We had "attempted great things for God." It had been "easier to take much than little"—and we again found that "all things are possible to him who believes" (Mark 9:23).

Now, as I sat with my friend and remembered that trip to Czechoslovakia, I pondered its meaning. Couldn't I trust God now for those same promises? Couldn't He show me once again how it would be "easier to take much than little?"

"Bill, what do you need?" My friend looked at me with concern. The Czech scenario had momentarily distracted me, and my friend's question returned me to the present with a jolt.

"I need a good, professional offset press," I said boldly.

"How much will it cost?"

"Oh, at least forty thousand dollars for a good secondhand machine," I told him.

For a few minutes my friend stared at the table, lost in thought. Then, his mind apparently made up, he looked at me and grinned. "Brother, you go ahead and buy that machine. I'll pay for it!"

I was stunned. Was my friend willing to contribute that sizable sum so I could purchase a new offset press? The smoldering hope in my heart came alive. A commercial press! At last we could begin making a dent in the enormous need for literature in Eastern Europe.

A few days later I met with SGA's general director, who was still in Europe. I could not contain my elation. "Guess what? Someone has volunteered to pay for an offset press! Will you allow me to buy it?"

He smiled and shrugged. "Well, if someone wants to pay for it—if the money is given for that project—what can I say? Go ahead; buy the machine."

So now I had $140,000 to spend: $100,000 previously delegated at the field-council meeting and the $40,000 donated by my friend. But I was shocked by the exorbitant prices the French charged for used printing equipment; a stitcher and a collator, the two machines that the field council had sanctioned, would cost me the entire $100,000 that SGA had allotted for that purpose.

I went to Holland, to a big secondhand printing machine shop that I knew of, and inquired about their offset machines. I had already been advised by a professional printer to try to find a good secondhand two-color T. P. Miller offset perfecting press. (This could print either two colors on one side of the paper or one color on each side of the paper simultaneously. This meant it could handle four-color work.) But this shop didn't have that kind of machine on hand. They did have a thirty-eight–inch, one-color Roland press. Since it was better than our present machine, I decided to order it, even though it wasn't exactly what I wanted.

Suddenly I realized that if I ordered that press, all my present printing equipment would be obsolete. I would immediately need bigger machines to go along with the bigger press. A new folder, another collator, a different stitcher, a bigger trimmer, a bigger camera, a bigger plate burner, roller washers—I would need them all. I would also need additional personnel trained to work with this equipment. Like it or not, I was caught in a vicious cycle if I wanted to move up to the next level of printing.

Fortunately this shop had secondhand editions of the new machines I would need. I was amazed that in Holland I could order everything except the press for the price the French shop wanted for only the stitcher and collator. What a bargain! I could save thousands of dollars buying the equipment in Holland. So I ordered the whole gamut needed to go into professional printing.

Two days after I returned to France I had a phone call. It was the manager of the big shop in Holland where I had ordered all my equipment. "Mr. Kapitaniuk, I found you a two-color perfecting press, a thirty-eight–inch T. P. Miller. Do you want to buy it?''

A two-color T. P. Miller was exactly what I had wanted all along. I was ecstatic! "How much does it cost?"

"Seventy thousand dollars."

My ecstasy shriveled. "Well, I haven't got the money," I began. Then quickly I added, "But don't sell it to anyone else! I'll get back to you." I hung up and immediately dialed the friend who had donated the forty thousand dollars for a used press. "Brother," I said when he answered the phone, "I've got a problem. I've found a two-color press, which would speed up our operation, but I don't know what to do."

"What's it going to cost you?"

How did he know the problem was money? "About seventy thousand dollars."

"Seventy thousand?" The question was very matter-of-fact, his voice free of emotion. There was silence for a few moments. Then the voice came back: "Go ahead and buy it. I'll pay for it."

I thanked him, hung up, and phoned the shop in Holland. "Okay," I said to the manager, "Cancel the order for the Roland, and I'll order that T. P. Miller from you."

Our saga of professional printing had finally begun. At that time I had no idea that it would be over a year before we could even begin printing, because trained personnel were hard to find. Or that a new multitude of headaches awaited us. Or that, once we began to print, we would turn thirty tons of paper into gospel literature for Eastern Europe in a mere twelve months. All I knew was that at last we had a decent press and could now print books on a large scale for Eastern Europe.

As I anticipated our plunge into the professional printing world, the need for literature did not abate but instead intensified. No more clearly was this need underscored than at a meeting of Polish Catholics that I had decided to attend. I surveyed the gathering with a slight feeling of unease. Most of my contacts in Poland were evangelicals, and I wasn't sure what to expect from this group of Roman Catholics. But I knew I had to come, once I heard of this special meeting being held by Polish Catholics interested in studying the Bible.

The interest, I was sure, had stemmed from the Catholic renewal movement in Poland. People were searching for spiritual fulfillment and were hungry to read the Word of God. Since 95 percent of Poles are baptized Roman Catholic, a renewal movement within the Catholic Church in Poland was significant. I had heard about it but, because of my limited involvement in Catholic circles, was unprepared for seeing the extent to which it had grown.

Suddenly a large, smiling priest emerged from the crowd and approached me. He clapped my shoulders between his enormous hands. "Mr. Kapitaniuk! How good of you to come!"

There was no mistaking that gray, balding head, that soft-spoken voice that I knew could become infused with power when exercised before a group. I nodded at him. "Father Andrzej! Nice to see you again." I smiled as I reflected on the impact that this quiet, gentle man was making throughout Poland. . . .

The "impact" began in the early 1950s. Father Andrzej and his colleagues, in an effort to counter the excessive atheistic indoctrination that the children in their diocese were getting in school, decided to develop a new type of retreat. Their main purpose was to portray the childhood of Jesus as it was expressed in purity, obedience, and love. Father Andrzej also wanted to give the boys a model of the Christian life to follow in their everyday lives, so the daily routine included prayer, reading the Bible, and writing thoughts on the passage read.

But what started as simple retreats for children blossomed into a full-scale Catholic renewal movement. By 1968, the movement— known as Oasis—was in full bloom. "By Oasis," said Father Andrzej, "I mean a particular method of spiritual exercises and teachings worked out over many years of experience and based on a personal encounter with God through Christ in the Spirit. During the fifteen days of the retreat, the participants learn to relate personally to God through the Bible, prayer, and worship. . . . This takes place in a spirit of mutual service, an attempt to live out *agape,* the selfless love modeled on the example of Christ."

In the 1970s, Oasis groups penetrated many local parishes, and the Oasis retreats spread rapidly throughout the country. In 1972, retreats for various groups—schoolchildren, university students, young workers, adults, priests, seminarians, and nuns—were organized. Then, in 1973, the first Oasis for entire families was organized. As people from more and more walks of life became involved, the movement skyrocketed; the number of participants grew from some 1,500 in 1968 to more than 30,000 ten years later.

In March 1976, during the first congress of Oasis leaders, the movement adopted a new name: Light-Life. In addition to a new name, the leaders adopted a new aim: all members of the movement, regardless of their age and status in the Catholic Church, should strive toward Christian maturity, not only through studying God's Word, the liturgy, and prayer, but also through witness and active service. The following summer, the first Oasis for evangelization took place.

During the summer of 1981, 45,000 Poles attended the Light-Life retreats, and eighty percent were young people between the ages of fifteen and eighteen. (In 1982, even more participated, despite the fact that martial law was then in force.) Afterwards they began to meet weekly in homes for Bible study and prayer. In these weekly meetings, they followed the recommended course of study: "Ten Steps to Christian Maturity." As they received additional Bible training and were invited to follow-up camps during the next two years, they received the specialized Bible training necessary for their lives of Christian witness and discipleship.

Nearly 300,000 people had participated in the Oasis/Light-Life retreats by 1984, and there were Light-Life groups in 2,000 parishes. And the movement continues to grow, although the evangelical emphasis has shifted.

As I was reflecting on what the Oasis movement had meant to the Roman Catholic Church in Poland, the 250 delegates from all over Poland had gathered to discuss their evangelization plans. I was impressed by their commitment, their enthusiasm, and their earnest desire to see all of their Polish countrymen have a personal encounter with Jesus Christ. One way they hoped to meet their goal was through a special evangelization project: a Western mission was providing them with eighty copies of the film *Jesus*. These gathered delegates' desire was to show this film to every possible Polish community.

But I soon learned that their plans were more involved than simply showing the film. At the conclusion of the day's session, Father Andrzej came up beside me, took me by the elbow, and steered me away from the crowd. "Mr. Kapitaniuk, we would like to have some Gospels of Luke in Poland."

Had he learned of my interest in printing? At this point, our T. P. Miller had been gathering dust for nearly a year because we couldn't find a printer. "How many do you need?" I asked naively.

"We'd like to have at least twenty million."

I stared at him in astonishment. Twenty million? He couldn't be serious! I cleared my throat. "You're not very realistic, are you?"

He looked genuinely shocked. "Oh, but we're being very realistic; we'd like to give one Gospel to every person who attends the film, because, as you know, the *Jesus* film is based on the Gospel of Luke. We're hoping that within a few years we can show this film to every person in Poland."

"Well, twenty million; that's rather difficult—" I tried hard not to sound negative; I didn't want to dampen his enthusiasm.

"If you could give us at least five million, we'd be very happy," he told me.

I shook my head doubtfully and stared at the ground, but I had to smile in spite of myself. Here was a man who, like me, appeared to see beyond obstacles. But where would I get twenty million—or even five million—Gospels of Luke? Even if I could begin a large-scale printing operation immediately, such an order would take years. I certainly wanted to help provide Scripture portions so that Polish Catholics could study God's Word. What an opportunity! But what could one man, such as I, possibly do for such a great need? And what of the myriad of other needs I knew of among the evangelicals?

A while later, on another trip to Poland, I discovered that my Catholic friends had secured a commercial printer to print some Gospels of Luke for them. But what a price they had to pay—forty cents for each Gospel. A scant one million copies, only a small fraction of what they really wanted, cost $400,000.

I had done enough printing to calculate the tremendous profit this commercial printer was making. I was reminded of the passage in First Samuel (13:19–21) where the Israelites had to go to the Philistines to sharpen their plowshares, axes, and other tools because the Philistines were so afraid of the Israelites making weapons that Hebrew blacksmiths had been exiled. I could just imagine what the Philistines would do in time of war, when they realized that those tools could be used against them! They certainly wouldn't do a good job of sharpening them. Once again I felt that we Christians often went to the world to "sharpen our tools," to print our

Christian literature. Why not print our own? I left Poland more determined than ever to find a way to begin a professional printing operation.

The sound of our T. P. Miller's rhythmic clacking and thudding lifted my spirits just as the notes of Handel's *Messiah* have thrilled the souls of many down through the ages. I picked up one of the completed pages as it came off the press—*Evangelical Speaking Pictures*, the Hungarian Pace book. I glanced around the room at our new folder as it methodically creased just the right places, at the collator as it spit out stacks of book sections in precise order, at the gluing machine as it glued the sections together, and at the cutter as it precisely cut each completed book. How different from our first attempts at printing this very book! I could only marvel at the Lord's provision.

The whole process seemed miraculous as I reflected on the years of perseverance and frustration it had taken to arrive at this point. I looked over at Lonnie, our printer, and smiled. Only the Lord could have put this operation together!

Lonnie had learned the printing trade from his father as he worked alongside him for several years. He graduated from college, however, with a premed degree and a desire· to continue his medical education. He managed a print shop for his old alma mater after graduation and took another position as a printer while taking graduate courses.

But, in March 1983, the door to a graduate program at the University of Nebraska Medical Center closed. And, as the Lord often does, He provided Lonnie and his family with another, totally different, opportunity: He showed them our need for a printer in Billy-Montigny, France. As Lonnie realized the unique ways the Lord had prepared both him and his wife, Debbie, he decided to accept the challenge and come to France as our printer.

Then there was Philippe, whose very presence here was nothing short of a miracle. He was our second-oldest son and had always been interested in the printing process. He began helping in the print shop when we had our older machines as he was finishing high school. He and Daniel, our eldest, began to work in the lab together developing pictures, doing the masking, burning the plates. Once his appetite was whetted, Philippe worked in the print shop during the day and for a year spent his evenings at night school studying professional printing. Besides the Pace book, we were busy printing material in French. Philippe actually conceived, designed, typeset, and printed a minijournal for the local French youth work.

But the fiasco when we first printed the Hungarian Pace book on our old A. B. Dick disillusioned and frustrated Philippe. I don't think he realized until then just how archaic our operation was. Far from excited about working with slow, antiquated presses that produced such poor-quality results, he decided to take some time off from printing and go to Bible school.

While on vacation from school in early 1982, Philippe had a diving accident similar to Joni Eareckson's; he broke his neck. But the Lord miraculously intervened, and, to the amazement of the doctors, Philippe is completely healed today with no paralysis! By the fall following the accident, Philippe was recovered sufficiently to resume classes.

By the time we started establishing our more sophisticated printing operation, Philippe could see the problems I would have as administrator, since I was also busy traveling to Poland as well as pastoring the church in Billy-Montigny. So he offered to manage the print shop for me, a real answer to prayer.

Meanwhile, Daniel had gone into teaching after he completed his education. He taught for five years, but he, too, was watching our developing printing venture with interest. One day he came to me and said, "Dad, I feel that I must quit my teaching for at least a year and come and help you."

I was delighted. "That's terrific!" I responded. So Daniel managed all the masking and lab photography work, things that he and Philippe had learned together on our old machines. How thankful to the Lord I was for Daniel! As a real perfectionist he would lend a professional expertise to our endeavors.

As I stood thinking about my two oldest sons, a slight young woman slipped through the door. She carried a baby and a young boy held her hand. She spotted her husband and approached him. I smiled as I thought how different this young couple was from when I had first met them. . . .

"Pastor, I was wondering if you could marry us?" Dominique, a petite, dark-haired young woman looked up at me with enormous eyes after the Sunday morning service.

"What?" Dominique's question caught me so completely off-guard that I blurted the response without thinking. She and her "husband," Allan, had arrived in Billy-Montigny several weeks earlier with their toddling young son, and it had never occurred to me that they weren't married. Our son David's friend, Dominique's brother, had asked if his "sister and her family" could come from Nice and stay with us. I had consented, and Allan began work in the print shop back when we had the A. B. Dick. He had impressed me as a hard worker.

In addition to impressing me, Allan had also surprised me when they had first arrived. With his dark eyes and long black hair, he looked like an American Indian! But he and Dominique had started coming to the Sunday meetings in our little French/Polish church, and Allan's interest in the gospel soon became evident when he began asking questions. After a while I noticed that Allan's hair was becoming progressively less shaggy, and one Sunday he arrived in church with short hair! Now, about four months after they had arrived in Billy-Montigny, Dominique was approaching me about marrying them.

Her face was so earnest, so sincere. I cleared my throat. "Usually, as a general principle, we don't marry people who aren't baptized; we marry Christians," I said gently.

"Well," she added, "we'd like you to baptize us!"

"But how can I baptize you if you are living together out of wedlock?" I asked. Red lights started flashing in my mind as I realized the impact this situation might have on the congregation. It could be scandalous in the church, provoking all sorts of cruel responses. I had to tread very carefully; I had no idea what to do. So

I prayed silently and in the end persuaded Allan and Dominique to have a civil wedding ceremony at the town hall and then a quiet, low-key reception at our youth center.

But I had to make their marriage public, so the following Sunday, during the announcements, I said, "Allan and Dominique were married yesterday." Before the shock had too much chance to register, I hastened to add, "We must remember how the apostle Paul said, 'and yet I was shown mercy, because I acted ignorantly in unbelief' (1 Tim. 1:13b). No doubt God has also forgiven Allan and Dominique, because they, too, acted in ignorance." Fortunately, the congregation agreed with my interpretation, and they accepted Allan and Dominique with open arms.

Some time later they were baptized, and they both worked in the print shop as we were getting started with our old equipment. But when Philippe left for Bible school, Allan and Dominique followed suit and went to Bible school for two years.

It so happened that as Allan and Dominique were finishing school, we were setting up our new printing equipment. They wrote to us, not knowing this development, and asked if they could come back and work with us. "Sure!" I responded. "We're going to begin our new printing operation." And they returned to carry on their work with the folder, collator, book binder, and cutter.

As Dominique stood speaking with Allan, another small woman strode into the room—Lucette. Her exuberance and love for life bubbled over into all she did, and her expertise was exactly what we needed. Lucette was yet another of the Lord's gifts to us.

From her mother we had learned that Lucette was fluent in French, German, and English, and that she was working as a secretary in Germany. I told her mother that we were looking for a secretary/bookkeeper in our new print shop and that Lucette sounded ideal.

One day Lucette was at home in France, visiting her mother, and the two of them came to the shop. I had a chance to explain our work to Lucette and to ask her to consider coming to work with us. I realized that for her to accept our

position would mean taking a great cut in pay. But she loved
the Lord, and she could see that our efforts in the print shop
were dedicated to His glory. So she left her work in Germany
to accept our position as secretary/bookkeeper.

And then there was Gilles. A short, husky man with a dark
beard and a twinkle in his eyes, he worked with Lonnie on the
press. Gilles was another of our "miracle workers." To look at
him now you would never guess that our first meeting with
him was anything but pleasant. . . .

Gilles had arrived at our youth center to take his children out of
a youth meeting. Allan had started a Bible club for the neighborhood
children, and Gilles, an ardent communist, was furious when he
heard that his children were attending the club. For many years he
had served as secretary for the Communist Party in various parts of
France, and he was now serving in that capacity in Billy-Montigny.

However, when he went down the stairs to the basement where
the meeting was being held, Allan began to talk with him. Allan has
a quiet, gentle manner, as well as determination, and Gilles listened.
He actually became interested in what Allan was saying and started
attending the youth meetings. Little by little his questions and
objections were answered and he gave his life to Christ!

Gilles' conversion by no means solved his problems, since he was
having serious financial difficulties at that time. He was 25,000 francs
in debt to the electric company; his electricity had been cut off for
some time already, and he had a little diesel generator to keep his
electrical appliances going. He also had a wife and eight children to
support. As a rule, the French government gives a "housing allowance" depending on how many children are in the family. But Gilles
was not receiving this allowance because he wasn't paying the rent
on his house. So he was in a desperate situation.

We tried to help him as best we could. I scratched together my
savings, and with help from the church we were able to bail him out
of his financial difficulties. We got his electricity and his housing
allowance going again, and his life continued on a more even keel.

Gilles was very grateful and wondered if he could do some
volunteer work in the print shop. "I've worked enough for the devil;

now I want to consecrate the rest of my life to the Lord," he told us. He worked in the shop for about a month, and we found him very useful, so I offered him a full-time job. He trained with Lonnie on the T. P. Miller. Gilles had never done printing before but learned quickly and could now handle the machine on his own except for minor adjustments. In fact, the pages of our second-edition Pace book looked great.

The rhythmic sounds of our printing machinery lulled me toward my age-old dreaming. For the black-and-white Pace book was only the first of several projects we had planned. We still had to work out some glitches in the T. P. Miller before we could begin printing four-color projects, and I had one that I could hardly wait to begin, one that I had first seen the need for years before, when a rotund figure in Warsaw gestured at a pile of letters heaped on the table and overflowing onto the floor. "In these letters, and in our files, there are requests for ten thousand copies of those *Life of Christ* books!"

I had stared with my mouth open. The Polish people had gone wild over this one book! I was then visiting Warsaw only months after we had delivered that first batch of seven thousand Polish *Life of Christ* books during the Solidarity Crisis. It was my first tangible proof of this book's impact, but it was certainly not the last. SGA headquarters in Wheaton, Illinois, informed me that letters were coming into their office from Poland almost every day asking for copies of the book. On a later trip to Poland, Roman Catholic leaders said to me, "We'd like to have ten thousand of your books for our church."

It began to dawn on me that there was no bottom to this need. Why, even if we could print these books ourselves for the rest of our lives, we would never saturate the country of Poland! It was then that I began to wonder whether there was some way we could begin to print these books in France.

"Brother, we really love this book, but it has problems." A dear Polish friend brandished a copy of *Life of Christ* before my eyes. This was later, when I was traveling in Poland during the time of martial law and had brought yet another shipment of the now-sought-after books. The SGA headquarters, reflecting on the gravity of the situation in Poland, had had an additional 50,000 copies of *Life of Christ* printed and shipped to Europe.

As my SGA co-worker and I listened, this Polish brother described some grammatical errors, language problems, and other technical faults in the first edition of our book. They wanted more of the books but asked if we could first correct these difficulties. He offered to find a Christian in Poland to edit the book, if we were willing. We agreed, telling our friend that it was now possible to add an additional segment to the existing *Life of Christ* so that the new book was virtually an illustrated New Testament. His face lit up as we offered to bring that segment to Poland to be translated.

Over the course of several months, the original *Life of Christ* was edited in Poland, and the additional segment translated. But then came a new problem: the words for the "balloons" (which indicated the speaking of the various characters) had been typed in our first edition, and we weren't completely satisfied with the effect. We hoped we might find a talented person who could hand-letter the words.

Once again we were eyewitnesses to the Lord's perfect preparation. Years before, I had attended the wedding of a Polish couple who now had a grown family. They were old friends and mentioned that their daughter was a graphic artist. Perhaps, they said, she could do the balloons for us. Of course, we wanted to see samples of her work, but we weren't disappointed; her work was excellent and we gave her the job. The finished product was a true work of art!

In my next communication with SGA headquarters, I asked for, and was granted, the privilege of printing the now-complete Polish *Illustrated New Testament.*

"We're almost done; only a few more pages to go!"
More than a year had passed since I had asked permission to print the Polish *Illustrated New Testament.* The room before me, in our print shop, was a hodgepodge of color and mate-

rial—special tape, film negatives, large sheets of orange paper, scraps strewn on the floor, special masking tools—but our 256-page *Illustrated New Testament* was almost masked and ready for the plates to be burned.

Preparing to print a project of this size was no simple task; it was our first four-color job. In the preparation process, all the pages were multiplied by four because a separate negative was needed for each color of each page—one for the blue, one for the black, one for the red, and one for the yellow. In addition, the colors had to line up correctly to produce the proper image. The negatives were each arranged and fastened onto a large sheet or flat, and then the images on the flats were burned onto metal plates, which received the ink from the press and transferred the images onto paper. Preparing almost 64 flats had taken nearly the whole month . . . .

While printing the Pace book on the T. P. Miller, Lonnie had found several things that weren't working properly—things that were minor irritations when working on a black-and-white job but would be greatly magnified on a four-color project. Realizing we needed some professional advice, he telephoned Back to the Bible Broadcast. Larey Kauffman, one of Back to the Bible's printers, had years of printing and management experience and agreed to come over to help us for a month. And his wife, Linda, was a godsend in sharing her experience in print preparation with Daniel. It was she, Daniel, and several others who nearly completed masking up the Polish *Illustrated New Testament* in the short month the Kauffmans were in Billy-Montigny.

Meanwhile, Larey had set to work helping us get our printing operation functioning at its maximum capacity. One of the first things he did was to rearrange machines to allow work to progress through the shop more efficiently. Then he and Linda helped regulate the equipment, including making repairs and adjustments on the T. P. Miller. Of course, Larey couldn't make these adjustments without running some of the *Illustrated New Testament* pages through the press so he could see the problems firsthand—what a joy to actually see those pages coming off our own press!

By the end of June 1984, when the Kauffmans went back to the States, we were ready to begin printing in earnest. And earnest we needed to be if we were going to deliver our first shipment of 25,000 Polish *Illustrated New Testaments* to Poland in September.

"How many tons?" Madame C. worked in the Paris office and was responsible for coordinating the dispatching of Polish trucks. She sounded quite professional on the telephone. During the next several months, I would become very familiar with her voice.

"At least fifteen."

"Good. When do you want the truck?" I could picture her taking down the information in a little notebook.

"On the twelfth."

"Good," she remarked again. "The truck will be there."

I hung up and smiled. Finally, after months of waiting, all the pieces were fitting together. We had our professional offset press and the printer to run it; we had the personnel we needed for all phases of the printing operation; we had printed our first 27,000 Polish *Illustrated New Testaments* and had permission from the Polish government to import them. And we had secured free transportation for these New Testaments in a Polish government truck!

But what a long road had led to this point. I would not soon forget the struggles, the frustrations, the setbacks of the past months. Now we were beyond the point of no return; at last we were in the printing business, where the Lord could multiply our feeble efforts.

I walked out into the huge room that housed our printing equipment and watched the *Illustrated New Testaments* in their final stage of preparation as they came out of the cutter. How beautiful were these books that told the gospel of our Lord Jesus! To me those books were pure gold; through printing them we had a part in doing something for eternity. And, once again, they were only a beginning. The Lord had even greater plans ahead.

12

Multiplying the Loaves and Fishes

All of Poland is asking for that one book, the *Illustrated New Testament*—" I stared at the letter before me, hardly able to believe my eyes. *All* of Poland? Yes, that was the expression he had used. I continued reading, "—my great regret is that I have only eighty copies left."

Barely three months earlier, in September, 1984, we had delivered our first shipment of 27,000 *Illustrated New Testaments* to Poland. How encouraging to hear that already it was being received so well! But how could one book so captivate a country in three months that so many people were suddenly clamoring for a copy?

I shook my head. The letter was from one of the Polish pastors who had received part of our shipment. How I felt for him! Even in the short time we were in Poland delivering those very books, we had seen several indications of how the book would be received. One incident involved the drivers of the Polish government truck that arrived at our doorstep in France to pick up the New Testaments; another, a customs official; and still another, a Communist Party member. I remembered them all in great detail. . . .

A muted September dusk was beginning to fall as my faded gold Citroen emerged from the bustling crowd of downtown Billy-Montigny and bumped across the railroad tracks. The narrow streets surged with people as they hurried to collect groceries for their evening meals. I swerved to avoid a bicycle, turned down an even narrower street, and drove in turn past a local elementary school, a bakery, and a meat market. A panorama of our area's slag heaps, towering over row after row of brick houses, lay silhouetted against the rosy sky ahead of me.

I made one more turn and caught my first glimpse of what I had been waiting months to see: the truck that would carry our first load of *Illustrated New Testaments* into Poland. The truck just fit into the wide, paved area in front of our youth center. As I drew closer, I could see bold red letters splashed across the bright yellow cab: PEKAES. There was no mistaking this vehicle: it was a Polish government truck.

The drivers were nowhere to be seen, so I turned onto the street near the truck, drove about a block, and pulled into our gravel driveway. I hopped out of the car, pushed open the back door of our house, and saw two young men seated at our dining-room table. They were engaged in an animated Polish conversation as they ate from plates piled high with steaming food. One of the men, a heavyset fellow with sandy hair, gestured constantly with his hands as he spoke. The other, dark-haired and of slighter build, seemed more reserved.

My gaze moved beyond this scene into the kitchen, and fell on Sophie hovering over the stove, wooden spoon in hand as she stirred something in a large aluminum pot. Steam had condensed on her wire-rimmed glasses, and her jaw was set in its typical resolute expression. A floral print dress hung limply from her broad shoulders and accented her obvious weariness. As I watched, she lifted the pot from the stove, carried it to the table and began ladling gravy over the mountains of rice on each man's plate. She caught sight of me and smiled. "Here's my husband now," she began in Polish.

At that, the two men turned toward me, and I thrust my hand toward the closer one and greeted him in Polish. It wasn't very often that we entertained Polish citizens in our home, and both Sophie and I felt privileged to have such an opportunity. I asked the men where they were from and about their families. They, in turn, seemed interested in our printing work and asked a lot of questions before I happened to glance at Sophie, who was motioning for me to go with her. So, as our new Polish friends finished their meal, I excused myself and followed Sophie into the kitchen.

Sophie grabbed my arm, her face beaming. "The Lord has given us a wonderful opening with these men," she began. "When they first arrived, we talked for a while and I asked if there was anything they needed. You see the heavyset one there? His daughter is very sick, and he told me he'd be very grateful if he could find the medicine that she needs. So before supper I dashed out and bought it." As usual, her French had become more rapid as her excitement rose.

"You found the medicine?"

"*Oui,* I found it and, as I came back, I was praying for a chance to talk about the Lord. When they sat down to eat, I said, 'Do you mind if I pray? Because we pray before we eat in this house.' So they said, 'No, we don't mind.' And, after that, they started asking questions about who we are and what we are doing, and I told them about the Lord and what He is doing with our printing. The one with the sick daughter, he was very open. I tell you, it's no accident that she is sick! The Lord knows about it. That's why they were so interested in talking about the printing when you came in."

Later I pushed open the back door and walked toward the print shop. I had just gotten our two new friends settled for the night. Sophie was right; they were both interested in talking about spiritual truths and we had had a good discussion. Truly, the Lord had directed them to us.

A hubbub of activity greeted me as I entered the print shop. Most of my sons (we now had eight sons: Daniel 26, Philippe 24, David 23, Paul 21, Joël 18, Jean 14, Samuel 12, and Timothée 8) and the print-shop workers were busy loading boxes with *Illustrated New Testaments* and tying them onto pallets. It was hard work to tie up eight tons of books, but the atmosphere was one of excitement—we had waited years for this moment! For the first time in our printing history, we were sending a shipment of books to Poland that we had actually printed ourselves on our own press and processed on our own machines.

Sophie and her sister Janine were busy stuffing box after box with clothes and medicines that had been donated for Poland. Then these, too, were tied onto pallets, along with some building materials we were taking in for a Polish congregation. Altogether, the clothes, medicines, and building materials weighed about seven tons; when these boxes were added to the New Testaments, our truck would carry a total of fifteen tons.

I walked over to where Sophie and Janine were working and touched Sophie lightly on the shoulder. "Do you know what those two truckers are asking for?" I said softly.

Sophie paused from her work and looked up at me expectantly, shaking her head.

"Bibles. They're both asking for Bibles," I told her.

"You mean *Illustrated New Testaments?*"

"No, they want whole Bibles!"

Sophie's eyes lit up and her smile widened. "Praise the Lord! It's no accident that they came here. The Lord sent them!"

"You must have some more soup." The Polish woman looked stern as she reached for my bowl, and then my brother-in-law George's, but I knew she was merely looking after us in typical Polish fashion. We would never escape from the table half-full if she could help it! After ladling our bowls to the brim and placing them back in front of us, she extended the plate of freshly cut bread toward me. The bowl of pickles, the sliced tomatoes, the plate of thinly sliced meat—all made the rounds again as we talked and laughed.

After all our hassles on the Polish border (see chapter 1), we had finally made it into Poland and were visiting with one of our Polish truck drivers and his family. We were amazed at how we had become friends with those two truckers literally overnight. Once the pallets were prepared, they had helped us load them onto the truck—heavy work—and impressed us with their friendly and cooperative spirit. Both of them asked us to stay with them once we arrived in Poland and, because of their spiritual interest, George and I had decided to make a special effort to meet with them.

"Do you have to go on right away? Can't you stay with us overnight?" the heavyset trucker with the sparse blond hair asked between mouthfuls.

"Oh, yes, stay!" His wife looked at us imploringly.

I looked from one to the other. Much though I would have enjoyed a longer visit, our border delay had cost us precious time; it was already Saturday. I shook my head. "I'm sorry, but we can't. We have a meeting tomorrow in Brzeg" (a town just over 100 miles away).

They nodded sadly. "Well, we'd better see about that battery of yours," the trucker added. Our car battery had died and our Polish friend thought he might be able to help. He and George and I got up from the table and walked outside. The truck driver found an extra battery, and in no time we had installed it and were ready to be on our way.

As we stood talking, his wife approached me. She fidgeted nervously with her apron. "Those books you're carrying, the ones for children, could I have some?" she asked quietly. "We have three married sons and they all have little children. I'd like very much to give each of my sons one of those books."

Rivulets of sweat streamed down my back and my chest as we heaved the last pallet of building materials from the truck. I glanced at the two truck drivers and at the men from the Polish church who had helped us; they looked as sticky and exhausted as I felt. I pulled a handkerchief out of my pocket and mopped my forehead. Seven tons of building materials and a pallet of books seemed heavier when fewer men were moving them than had loaded them in France! I leaned against the side of the truck to catch my breath.

A short, wiry man emerged from the church building and glanced around. When he saw me, he ambled slowly to my side. "Mr. Kapitaniuk, I didn't ask your permission, but as we were unloading that pallet of books I opened a box and took one for my grandson. I'd like to give it to him as a gift. I hope you don't mind."

I couldn't help but smile as I listened to him. A communist customs official wanting a New Testament! Whoever would have guessed? This little man had been assigned to us once our truck had finally reached Poznan (see chapter 1). When we finished unloading the building materials, the pastor had asked him to help with a pallet of *Illustrated New Testaments.* For some reason they appealed to him.

"I'd be very happy for you to have one," I said. "You know, I'm sure you'll agree with me that this is a better gift for our kids than some pornography or detective books."

He nodded. "You're right. This will do them much more good."

George rubbed his head and grinned at me as we sped along the bumpy country road. Our small car and Poland's dirt "highways" made bumps and jolts inevitable, and often our heads received the brunt of the rocks and potholes. Just that day, while we were visiting Warsaw, we discovered that church officials had scheduled a meeting for us in Wloclawek, nearly a hundred miles away. I had a lot of work in Warsaw, and couldn't get away till 4:45 that afternnon. The meeting in Wloclawek was scheduled for 6:00 P.M., so we tore like mad across the less-than-ideal roads.

But a hundred miles is a hundred miles, and by the time we reached the outskirts of Wloclawek we were already a half-hour late. I didn't have directions to the church either, just an address. So, as we came into town, I drove to where a bus was unloading and asked if anyone knew the street I was looking for. The first man off the bus didn't know, but at the far end of the line a woman's voice called out, "I know where it is!" She came up to us and said, "If you'll take me in your car, I'll show you."

Since the minutes were ticking by and we needed to get to the church, I responded without even thinking about it: "Okay. We'll make room for you in the car." We moved some of our stuff around and she climbed into the back seat.

Our new passenger was petite, blond, and looked about fifty or so. As the car began to move, she looked somewhat embarrassed. Nervously she played with a strand of her hair and said, "I'm sorry for my appearance. I worked in the hospital all last night and was sleeping all day; I just got up. I have an appointment to give an injection to a sick baby and I overslept. I didn't even have time to comb my hair. I hope you don't mind me the way I am."

We started talking with her and explained our predicament. In the course of our discussion, we handed her a copy of the *Illustrated New Testament*. She took it and started looking through it but didn't make any comment. After a minute or two she looked up and asked, "Could you take me to that baby's house? It will only take me three minutes to give the injection, and then I'll take you right to the church where you are going."

"Well, we're late already, so three minutes more or less won't make much difference," I said. So we drove her to the house and waited in the car while she dashed in to give the injection. She even left her purse in the car. A few minutes later she was back. "You didn't look in my wallet, did you?" she asked as she got back into the car.

"No, we aren't interested in that."

She gave us directions to the church and in no time we were there. We quickly piled out of the car. By now we were about forty-five minutes late. I turned to the woman. Since she was a nurse, I assumed she had other calls to make, so I handed her a package of coffee and thanked her for her help. "You know," I continued, "If you have a chance to come here, they have meetings on Sunday mornings, Sunday evenings, and Wednesday evenings, like today."

She had to crane her neck to look up at me. "Well, can I come today?"

"Sure you can. Are you free?"

"Yes."

We all rushed into the church. Just as I walked through the door, the pastor was stepping up to the platform. He had lost hope of our coming and was about to begin speaking. But he caught sight of me and called, "Okay, Brother Kapitaniuk. Come here and start preaching!"

So I went right from the car to the pulpit, without a minute to catch my breath. I gave a message and afterwards we were invited for tea and cookies. As I walked to the back of the church, the nurse was standing at the book rack, picking up several books and thumbing through them. She came over to me with two in her hand. "Can I take these?" she asked me.

She was holding a Bible and a hymnbook. "You'll have to ask someone from the church here," I responded.

She inquired and they gave the two books to her. But she seemed uneasy and started toward the door. I went over to her. "Why don't you stay for a cup of tea with us?"

"I'm a stranger. I don't know anybody."

I wondered whether it was fear I read in her expression. "We're all strangers," I assured her.

Finally she sat down, her dark eyes fleeting from face to face. Then she cleared her throat and spoke: "Before I eat, before I drink, I'd like to introduce myself. I'm a member of the Communist Party and have been for the last thirty-seven years. I'm an atheist; I don't believe in God." Now she had everyone's attention and drew several of us into a discussion. She was full of questions. Since she was a nurse, the first one was no surprise. "Tell me, how could Jesus be born without a human father? I went to school, I studied, and there are no such things as babies without fathers."

"Well," I said, "you have to take God into consideration. He is beyond the laws of nature. It was through the Holy Spirit that Jesus Christ was conceived, not through a human father."

Our conversation went on for a long time. Many of the woman's questions concerned miracles and the "impossibility" of various things that the church preaches. For example, the bodily resurrection and life after death didn't make any sense to her. "How can it be possible?" she asked. "Once you're dead, you're dead; there's no life after death."

The questions continued to flow, and I wondered just how much she was absorbing from our discussion. Yet I knew that our meeting her must have been of the Lord—our being late, her being on that bus after oversleeping—and that God would fit the puzzle together. She did take the Bible and hymnbook. George and I were rejoicing that she also took a copy of the *Illustrated New Testament*—she who had been an atheist and a communist for thirty-seven years! Even in the midst of her questions, I knew she was seeking, because at one point she told me, "You know, I don't believe in God. But I don't believe in communism either."

"All of Poland is asking for that book!" The Polish pastor's words echoed in my mind. Those recent instances—the two truck drivers, the customs official, the communist nurse— were early evidence that Poland was ripe to receive the *Illustrated New Testament*. I was well aware of how the printed Word of God could penetrate hearts. I had seen Bibles in Poland that were forty and fifty years old, Bibles that were still being used. Preachers' messages and radio programs were effective, but they could be heard only once. Books, on the other hand, could be read and reread. They could span generations and speak to thousands more people than I could ever touch in my lifetime.

As more and more copies of the *Illustrated New Testament* reached Poland, more and more requests for them filtered, then flooded, out to us. More than ever I was convinced that this book was one of the best tools we have today for evangelizing the communist world. Through the *Illustrated New Testament*, SGA could play a great part in evangelizing Eastern Europe.

Even my high hopes for the *Illustrated New Testament* seemed puny, however, when the Lord gave me a glimpse of how He would go far beyond my expectations in using them. This time, Sophie shared my joyful experience. . . .

The French countryside sped past our TGV window as Sophie and I settled into our seats. The TGV, a modern train reaching speeds up to 165 mph, was ideal, since we needed to get to Switzerland fast. I glanced over at Sophie and smiled. I knew she was in for a treat. For several months now, friends of ours in Switzerland had been holding unique month-long camps for Polish children, and Sophie had never visited them before this.

"Did you say seventy children?" I had asked my friend Jean André. Static, so typical of long-distance phone calls, crackled periodically on the line.

"Yes, and they have no New Testaments. Do you think you could send some quickly?" Jean's voice was tinged with a note of urgency.

"No problem; I'll deliver them myself."

I hung up the phone, explained the situation to Sophie and hurried upstairs to pack a small bag with my things. Usually I had to make these trips alone, so I was pleasantly surprised when Sophie approached me and said, "You know, I want to go and see those children from Poland."

"Great! We'll go together." After filling a large suitcase with about a hundred *Illustrated New Testaments*, we headed for the train station.

We arrived in Switzerland in the afternoon, while the children were out for a hike in the mountains, and had ample time to look over the grounds and wander through the buildings. The large dining room of the camp was empty, but Sophie and I could hear the kitchen clatter and bustle of preparation for the evening meal.

War-torn German refugee children from World War II, children from the poor areas of today's France, orphans, handicapped, extremely gifted children living in hard situations—all had found temporary refuge and solace here from their everyday struggles. In addition to the German and French children, British, Austrian, Greek, Italian, Jewish, Lebanese, and now Polish children had been loved and cared for in a Christian atmosphere of love and hope.

What a lovely setting for the camp Jean and his wife, Mady, had organized! The lush mountainside with its crisp air and picturesque views would soothe troubled hearts and minds. And the light, cheerfully decorated house had a homey atmosphere and lots of space, which would be attractive to any child. I also knew that the food was excellent and that the helpers were good-natured, kind, caring people. Yes, a perfect place for troubled children. I was lost in such thoughts as Jean approached and extended his hand.

"Mr. Kapitaniuk! It's good to see you! Thank you for coming." He turned toward Sophie. "And how nice that Mrs. Kapitaniuk could come along, too."

How I had grown to love this soft-spoken little man who had done so much for the children of Poland! As he stood smiling, sunlight from a nearby window shining on his sparse white hair, I conjectured that many people would be surprised to learn that this highly successful businessman had given so generously of his means and time to help thousands of children across Europe. I remembered how this unique refuge came about. . . .

Jean and Mady André had purchased two large, sturdily built homes in the Swiss mountains many years before. The first was intended as an orphanage, until the area's residents made it clear that they didn't want an orphanage in their village. After the war, Jean invited German children to come stay in the home, to refresh their spirits after the horrors they had so recently witnessed. Then, after the second home was purchased, the Andrés invited children from all over Europe. They and their dedicated staff fed the children, took them for hikes in the mountains, gave them new clothes, played games, taught them their schoolwork, gave them Bible lessons— and simply loved them. Some services, food, and clothing were donated, but the bulk of the expenses was covered by the Andrés' generosity.

In 1981 Jean left for a trip to South America and asked his wife to try to find some children to stay in one of their homes, which had been empty all fall. Mady had read about an organization in Zurich that was helping individual Polish children come to Switzerland for vacations; the children were placed in the homes of Swiss families. This was taking place during the Solidarity Crisis, when the Polish government greatly appreciated material assistance. But the gesture of goodwill had one serious problem: almost no Swiss family could communicate in Polish.

Madame André phoned the organization to see if it was possible to have a group of Polish children come to stay with them. The organization said that yes, this was possible, and Mme. André set about getting things prepared. By this time, the Andrés had hosted many of northern France's poor children in their homes. Jean's secretary remembered that "there's a man in Billy-Montigny who knows Polish; perhaps our friends in Lille could put us in touch with him." I turned out to be the "man in Billy-Montigny" and was able to help make the necessary arrangements in Poland and also to arrange for Polish-speaking people from France and Belgium to go to the Swiss camps to help.

Two months after Mady's phone call to Zurich, ninety-one Polish children arrived for a one-month stay in Switzerland! Three Polish officials accompanied them, as well as nine "group leaders." The children were the "cream of the crop," many of them coming from private Catholic schools and some from Polish orphanages. Two women taught Bible lessons and Christian songs; after only two weeks, more than half of the children had made personal commitments to Jesus Christ.

The Andrés found the Polish children particularly charming. They could never seem to get enough of the Bible teaching and even read during their free time. In addition, they were very polite and obedient, and their eagerness to learn warmed the hearts of the house workers. Brother and Sister André were able to make their own arrangements for subsequent groups of Polish children, and I helped with the details. The agreement was that the government would send 50 percent of the children and the Polish evangelical church would send the other half. Both Polish evangelical workers and government officials would accompany these groups.

When Jean first started his camps, we had not yet begun our printing operation but could send him copies of *Life of Christ* that had been printed in the States. By 1984, we had our own *Illustrated New Testament* and sent as many as possible to these children in Switzerland.

What had been a quiet, empty dining room that afternoon was alive a few hours later with laughing, chattering children and the sound of silverware scraping the plates for the last morsels of food from the evening meal. Jean André stood and introduced me briefly; as he sat down, I hauled my heavy suitcase to the center of the room.

I looked around at the expectant faces and asked, "How many of you here have big muscles?" Several hands shot up. "Can you lift this suitcase?" Nods and voices calling, "Yes!" "Of course!" "I can do it!" filled the room.

One by one they came up to grab hold of my suitcase and try to lift it. They grunted and groaned, but no one could budge it. Finally, one husky fellow stepped over and lifted it, but he was the only one who succeeded.

"What do you think is in that suitcase?" I asked.

"Rocks!"

"Nope," I replied.

"Food?"

"No." I grinned.

"I don't know—but it's heavy!"

"What's in it? Tell us; we give up!"

I stooped down and unfastened the clasps. As I lifted the top of the suitcase, all the children were on their feet, craning their necks for a glimpse. I pulled out a few copies of the *Illustrated New Testament* and a great "Oooo-ooooo-ooo!" sounded in the room. As Sophie and I started giving them out, the children could hardly contain their excitement. They had probably never seen a full-color book like this, especially a children's book. We made sure that everyone received a copy. Soon it was time for the children, and for us, to head to bed.

The next morning, a group of irate teachers confronted me. One balding man with dark-rimmed glasses glared at me. "You're really causing problems!" he exclaimed.

"What do you mean, 'causing problems'?"

"Last night we couldn't get the kids to sleep. They were hiding under the bed sheets with their flashlights, reading those New Testaments until midnight! And this morning, when they came to breakfast, we couldn't get them to eat because they were too busy telling each other what they had read in their books last night."

Sophie and I were thrilled to think that these kids, probably for the first time in their lives, saw something so interesting and so beautiful that they couldn't go to sleep. They couldn't even eat their breakfast because of their excitement!

That evening we met with the government officials who had accompanied the children from Poland to Switzerland. They were very pleased with what we were doing for their

children. One man looked at me and remarked, "We're happy that our children can spend their time here because it is doing them a lot of good."

We had developed some good contacts with these officials because of our involvement with the children. They knew we were really interested in the country, because there we were, during the problems of the Solidarity Crisis, sponsoring hundreds of their children for a stay in Switzerland, keeping them for a whole month, feeding them well, and sending them back safely. The Andrés paid for their airfare and supplied the children with almost one hundred pounds of food and clothes when they returned to Poland.

A short time later, I was in Poland and stopped to visit one of the government officials who had been very helpful, to leave her some coffee and chocolates. I had met her in Switzerland with the children, so when I stepped into her Polish office she was very excited to see me. In fact, she was bubbling over with such gratitude for what the Andrés and I were doing for the Polish children that she rushed over and kissed me. "This is for what you are doing for our Polish children!" she blurted. It gave me just a little picture of how appreciative the Polish people are—imagine a government official kissing a missionary!

By early 1986, eight hundred fifty Polish children had stayed with the Andrés in Switzerland, and many more are expected in the future. Jean told me that in the average groups of European children that come, 10 to 40 percent make decisions for Christ. In the Polish groups, however, this percentage is much higher: at least 50 to 60 percent of the Polish children decide to follow Jesus Christ. I saw this firsthand in a visit to one of Jean's camps in late 1985, where I spent some time just talking with the children.

One little twelve-year-old girl looked up at me with tears in her eyes as she said, "My father abandoned me when I was just three months old. My mother died a year ago. Nobody loves me."

Another little girl, only seven, grasped my hand. "My father was a drunk. I often begged him, 'Please don't drink!' One day he hanged himself in the doorway because my grandmother wouldn't give him money to buy whiskey. My mother was forced to go to work, and so my sister and I have to be in an orphanage."

"My mother used to work in the orphanage where I stayed when my father was in prison," another child told me. "One day my father was released. He got drunk, came to the orphanage, and beat up my mother. Mother was dismissed from her job. Now they quarrel every day. My father told Mother that one day he will kill her and then hang himself."

The forty-four children then at Jean's camp in Switzerland seemed so despondent this time. Eighteen of them were from a government orphanage, and many of these were submerged in sorrow or crushed under a load of grief. Nothing seemed to interest them. For hours, I listened as they poured out their souls to me.

I wondered what I could do. How could I comfort them? After a week, I returned to France and shared my burden with Sophie and our own children. After thinking and praying about the situation, I thought of a possible plan. I went to a department store and purchased crayons, pencils, pens, balloons, dolls—gifts for every child—stuffed them all in a huge suitcase and returned to Switzerland. Although I knew that toys and gadgets would not bring lasting peace, joy, and satisfaction to young, disillusioned hearts, I knew something else that could.

We spent time with the children, listening to them, hugging them, and loving them. Then we gave each child a New Testament, and I began to write the references to fifty Bible verses on a blackboard. I had especially chosen verses such as John 1:12, John 3:16, and John 5:24 because of the message they had for troubled souls.

After that, the children looked wide-eyed as I opened my suitcase of gifts. "Whoever learns the most verses will have the first choice of gifts," I said. But the greatest incentive to memorize Bible verses came when I showed them copies of the full-color *Illustrated New Testament.*

Everyone memorized, including staff people from the government orphanage. And, as they studied God's Word day after day, God's love and light penetrated their darkened hearts. By the time they returned to Poland, almost every child had had a personal experience with Jesus Christ. Even in the midst of the bitterness and disillusionment that many of these young lives had felt, I could see that Jean André was right: the Polish children seemed to be more open to the gospel.

As they were getting ready to leave, one child approached me. "I didn't want to come here," she said.

"Are you sorry you did come?" I asked gently.

She smiled. "Oh, no, because I found God here; I accepted Jesus Christ. Now I'm really glad that I came." A slight frown creased her brow. "Oh, I wish Jesus Christ came for us tonight. I don't want to go back to the orphanage!"

When the bus arrived to take the children to the airport, they all began to cry. They hugged us and thanked us for what we did and for what we gave them. As the bus drove down the mountainside, I could still hear the words that several children had spoken to me: "I like all that you gave me, Uncle, but the most precious gift that I received was the *Illustrated New Testament.*"

By the end of 1985, we had sent over 100,000 "missionaries" into Poland, in the form of *Illustrated New Testaments.* In twelve months we had produced and expedited these fearless and effective messengers. Now, all across Poland, in thousands of homes, they are bearing witness to children, youth, parents, and grandparents. They have been accepted by border guards, highway patrolmen, and government officials. But, as one priest said to me, "A hundred thousand copies for a land of thirty-six million is a drop in the ocean. We need one million of these New Testaments!"

Yes, we need many more New Testaments in Poland. But when I had feebly asked for free Polish government transport

for the initial ten thousand Bibles, the Lord graciously opened
the way for transporting more than ten times that amount.
And that door remains open. I can only believe that He is still
in the business of multiplying the loaves and fishes for those
who are hungering after Him.

13

"The Way . . . and the Truth, and the Life . . ."

What does that sign on your car say?" The middle-aged man shielded his eyes from the sun as he pointed to a large board fastened to the luggage rack on top of my car. It was a warm summer day in Wroclaw, in 1964, and a crowd had gathered as I was in a nearby building exchanging money.

I smiled. He was one of the first in Poland to remark about my unorthodox luggage carrier. Actually, I hadn't thought much about it when I had left France, but I now recalled the events leading up to the man's question. . . .

"They look great!" I announced, standing back to admire the artist's handiwork. Two large, flat boards, each about five feet long and a foot wide, stood drying in the sun. The bright yellows, reds, and blues were exactly what I wanted.

In the early 1960s, as a means of outreach, I had begun setting up a Bible stand in the French open markets. To carry my things, and also for publicity, I had an artist paint two big boards that I fastened to both sides of the luggage rack on top of my car.

On each board was a Bible text. One read, "Jesus said . . . 'I am the way, and the truth, and the life; no one comes to the Father, but through Me' " (John 14:6), and the other, "For the wages of sin is death, but the free gift of God is eternal life in Christ Jesus our Lord" (Rom. 6:23).

On market days I would travel from one market to another, putting up my table and selling Bibles. As the French vendors would call out, "Bananas!" or "Beefsteaks!" I would call out "Bibles!" And I was able to sell many Bibles at those open markets.

It was shortly after I had installed my new "evangelism boards" that I received a visa for Poland. I packed all my baggage on top of that rack. The luggage was very heavy, and the boards on the sides kept my bags together, so I left the texts on my car and went off to Poland. When I arrived at the border, officials looked at the signs but said nothing; the texts were in French, and the men probably didn't understand the language. So I passed through customs without a hitch, a rare border crossing for me, and was soon in the heart of Poland.

I stopped in Wroclaw and exchanged some money. When I returned to my car, several people were milling around it. One man said, "I'm a journalist from Denmark. Could you give me your address in France?" So I pulled a little gospel tract from my pocket, "The Way of Salvation," and wrote my name and address on it. Someone else asked for my address, so I did the same thing. It was then that the man approached me about one of the signs on my car rack. . . .

Now I glanced at the Polish man and then read, "Jesus said . . . 'I am the way, and the truth, and the life; no one comes to the Father, but through Me.' "

If I had punched the man, I don't think it would have infuriated him more. His face turned purple and his muscles tensed as he glared at me. After several seconds, he growled through clenched teeth, "And you think you're going to get to heaven in your car?"

I looked at him calmly. "Well, sir, if you don't repent, and if you don't accept Jesus Christ, you won't get to heaven by foot."

Before I finished speaking, three policemen had surrounded me. One wanted to see my passport. Another asked, "What are you doing here? What are you distributing?"

"Nothing," I replied.

"Yes, you are; you're distributing literature," he insisted.

"Oh," I said, as I remembered the tracts with the addresses, "I just gave some addresses to a few of these people."

The officer with my passport touched my arm. "Okay, come with us. Get into the car."

They drove me to the police station in Wroclaw, and before I knew it, I was standing before the chief of police. He looked me up and down. Then he asked. "Do you have a permit to bring those boards with the texts into the country?"

I shook my head. "No. They never said anything at the border. They let me through."

"You have to have a censorship permit to have such texts on your car."

I shrugged. "Well, no one told me."

He asked to see some of the tracts I had, then he and some others took them in to another room. After studying them for about an hour, they emerged. "You have to have a permit from the censorship department for those things—for the pamphlets and for your sign boards."

"Where do I get it?"

They told me where the censorship office was located and released me. I went back to my car and drove to this office, but it was closed for the day. That evening I went to a church meeting, and the next morning I presented myself at the censorship office again. This time it was open, and a man looked up from his desk as I walked in. "What do you want?"

"I want a permit for the two texts that I have on my vehicle."

"Are they printed or written?" he asked.

"They're written out by hand." I replied.

"We're not interested in what's *written*; we're only interested in what's printed."

So I left the office and traveled for a couple of months across Poland with those Bible texts. Wherever I stopped my car, I was always successful in drawing a crowd because everybody wanted to know what those texts said! The Lord used those boards in a wonderful way to bring people together so that I could talk about Him. And I learned in a fresh way that God's Word will not return to Him void.

That was more than twenty years ago. Over and over again, I have been reminded that the Lord often uses unique methods to bring His Word to those who need it in Eastern Europe. There have been times, of course, when this work has not been easy, and many times when I wondered exactly what God was doing. Recently, I was reading Song of Solomon, which says:

> "Awake, O north wind,
> And come, wind of the south;
> Make my garden breathe out fragrance,
> Let its spices be wafted abroad.
> May my beloved come into his garden
> And eat its choice fruits!" (4:16).

I have come to see that God has to send us the cold north winds as well as the burning south winds. We need both to bring out the fragrance in our lives, to break the alabaster boxes of our selves so that the fragrance will waft as a pleasing aroma before the Lord.

In Eastern Europe, a valiant church has emerged from this unique mixture of north and south winds. And the Lord has seen fit to give me the opportunity to bear witness to the growth of that church, to see God's Word work in the hearts of Slavic people, especially in Poland. Many times I have been reminded of a passage in Psalms:

> May the LORD answer you in the day of trouble!
> May the name of the God of Jacob
>   set you securely on high!
> May He send you help from the sanctuary,
> And support you from Zion!
> May He remember all your meal offerings,
> And find your burnt offering acceptable!
> May He grant you your heart's desire,
> And fulfill all your counsel! (Ps. 20:1-4).

In so many ways the Lord has answered me, has sent me help, has granted me my heart's desires. Through my times in Eastern Europe, the Lord has brought me to a place of great joy. Whenever I have caught glimpses of His working, He has given me a deep personal satisfaction in serving Him, a knowledge that He is using me in a small way to be an instrument through which He can work. Sometimes that satisfaction would come when I was traveling in Eastern Europe and someone would say to me, "Brother, this word that you brought was just exactly what I needed."

Other times He encouraged me in more dramatic ways. For example, I remember one Yugoslavian town where I was greeted on a wintry day by childish cries of "American preachers! American preachers!"

I rubbed my sleeve against the frosty car window and cleared a spot so I could see who was making the commotion. Children, bundled against the cold, were running up and down the streets announcing our arrival.

A Yugoslav friend and I were speaking in several areas of Yugoslavia and had planned a weekend of meetings here in the western town of Duga Resa. On Thursday we had sent a telegram to let the church know we would be arriving on Saturday. But the unpredictable winter weather interfered: a blizzard dumped two feet of snow on that part of the country, and we arrived before the telegram did.

The delayed telegram didn't matter, however, because the children had thoroughly heralded our arrival. Our first service that Saturday evening was packed! We had a terrific time together, and then the next day I spoke to a full church for three meetings—morning, afternoon, and evening.

By Sunday evening I was exhausted from travel, from preaching, and from constantly answering questions during the meal hours. So I preached to a crowded church for an hour and sat down. No sooner had I found my chair when a man stood up at the back of the church. "Sir, could you preach again? I came in late."

I had never heard of such a thing—someone asking me to bring the message *again*! Nothing like this had ever happened to me before. Reluctantly I pulled myself from my chair and walked wearily to the podium. I spoke for nearly forty-five mintues and then walked to the back of the church to shake hands with the people.

The crowd thinned, but about twenty-five people remained. An older gentleman approached me with a request: "Brother, we have questions. Can't you stay for a while yet?" We pulled some chairs into a circle, and one by one they fired questions at me. As I had found in many Slavic churches, their chief concerns were the signs of the times and the return of Christ.

After some time, I asked, "How many of you here are ready to meet the Lord if He should come? As far as I'm concerned, He can come any time to take His church out of this world. There is nothing in Scripture that tells us that He can't come today." I paused, then added softly, "How many of you are not ready, should the Lord come tonight?"

Two elderly ladies raised their hands and shook their heads as they murmured, "We're not ready."

Of all the people in that group, I certainly hadn't expected those women to respond! But I nodded and said, "Let's get down on our knees and pray, and you ask Christ to forgive you and come into your heart. The Bible says that if we confess our sins, He is faithful and just to forgive us our sins and to cleanse us from all unrighteousness. The Bible also says that he who hath the Son hath life. While you pray, you confess, and then by faith you accept Jesus Christ into your heart as your Savior."

We all knelt down and began to pray. As the two older ladies confessed their sins, their honesty before God and those people produced a chain reaction. What started as a question-and-answer session turned into a dynamic prayer meeting. We got down on our knees at 8:30 P.M. and didn't get off them until 1:30 A.M.!

A week later, I was having my final Sunday service in Yugoslavia, in a town about a hundred miles from Duga

Resa. After I finished my message, out of the corner of my eye I saw an elderly lady rushing toward the pulpit. Her gnarled face radiated joy as she clasped my hand in both of hers. Behind her spectacles, her eyes searched mine for recognition. "Brother Kapitaniuk, do you remember me?"

Silently I studied her face. I had met so many new people on this trip. She looked familiar, but—. I responded, "I've seen you somewhere, but I don't remember when or where."

"I was one of those ladies who prayed in Duga Resa. When I heard that you were leaving our country, I said to myself, 'I should go hear Brother Kapitaniuk preach one more time.' So I took the train."

I was humbled to think that someone was willing to travel nearly a hundred miles on a slow train just to hear me preach one message. I could understand traveling so far to hear someone like Billy Graham, but not to hear a country preacher like me. I was also humbled to think that the Lord was willing to work through me in such a way. In the midst of problems and frustrations, such instances reminded me of the Lord's presence and that He was fulfilling His promises in Scriptures such as Psalm 20.

The Lord especially blessed me again during a recent visit to Poland, when I was shown that seeds of faith planted by a long-ago sermon had flourished over the years in at least one believer. . . .

The Sunday-morning crowd dwindled as I stood by the door greeting people as they left the service in that Polish town. From the few who were still there, a wizened old lady emerged and tottered toward me. A dark shawl draped her thin shoulders and a black kerchief was tied under her chin. Because of her advanced years—probably eighty-five or so—she moved slowly, carefully, but at last she reached my side. She grasped my hand and said quietly, "Brother, I remember when you spoke in our church twenty years ago."

"What did I speak about?" I asked.

She smiled, her dark eyes sparkling. "You spoke about the man who lost his axe head."

As soon as she mentioned the subject, I remembered—"the man who lost his axe head" in 2 Kings 6:1–7. Suddenly the whole scene came back to me, and I remembered what I had said. . . .

"As the sixth chapter of Second Kings unfolds, we find a man cutting wood. Now, he wasn't involved in anything wrong; he was involved in a good thing for the Lord. He was doing his part to build and expand the work of God. And then, right in the midst of all that activity, of all that work, he lost his axe head.

"I believe that the axe head in this narrative represents power and effectiveness, and we see from the story that we can lose it right in the midst of service or activity. When the man lost his axe head, he lost his power, he lost his effectiveness to do the task at hand.

"Now, the first thing that we need to do when we lose our power is to stop working. A lot of Christians lose their axe head but keep making a lot of noise by beating the tree with their axe handle. It looks as if they are doing a terrific thing, but they aren't accomplishing much.

"Once we've quit swinging, once we've acknowledged that we've lost our power, then we must acknowledge that the power was not our own to begin with; it was 'borrowed.' That's what the man did. He cried out, 'Alas, my master! For it was borrowed' (v. 5). The Holy Spirit's power is given to us. It's from the Lord and not of us. We need to keep asking for a constant filling of that Spirit to be effective.

"The wonderful thing to keep in mind is the miracle that takes place next. When Elisha threw the branch into the water, the axe head swam. That is the miracle of the cross, that in spite of the fact that we lose our power, we can regain it if we, by faith, stretch out our hands and take what the Lord gives. Once the axe head floated, Elisha said to the man, 'Take it up for yourself.' And the man 'put out his hand and took it' (v. 7). If we're walking with the Lord, all we need do is simply ask the Lord to fill us with His Spirit and His power."

For the woman to remember that sermon after twenty years indicated that the message found its mark. Yes, the Lord was encouraging me as I went along.

And the Lord was also faithful in showing me future possibilities for service. . . .

"You want me to preach in *Ukrainian*?" I was in Canada for a brief visit during the fall of 1984 and had stopped to see friends in Edmonton. One asked me if I would speak in the Ukrainian church there on Saturday night, Sunday morning, and Sunday afternoon. Three Ukrainian meetings—and I hadn't used my Ukrainian for years!

I really sweated out the first meeting; I was so used to Polish and French that I had a hard time getting my tongue to form the correct Ukrainian words. The second meeting was better, but I was still struggling. By the third meeting, however, my tongue had loosened up and I sailed right along.

After the service, the pastor, a friend who had just been in the Ukraine that summer, approached me. "Bill, you know what those pastors in the Ukraine said to me? 'Come back! Minister! We have three thousand churches waiting for somebody to come and minister the Word of God!' " For some reason, he was looking at me imploringly.

I looked at the pastor steadily. He had originally come from the Ukraine, as had my parents. "Well," I asked, "why are you here in Canada? Why don't you go there and minister?"

His eyes fell. "I'm married and have the responsibility of the church here, Bill. I can't be spending a lot of time in the Soviet Union. And then there's the cost; it's expensive traveling back and forth from Canada to the Ukraine. It's a long trip!"

I nodded. His arguments were understandable—for him. But what about me? I lived much closer to the Soviet Union. The Ukrainian language I had spoken as a child had come back much faster than I would have thought possible. If I could go to the Ukraine and spend a couple of weeks there, I was sure I would have my original grasp of the language back again.

And what about my relatives? I realized that I had neglected trying to get the gospel to my own family in the Ukraine. Maybe I should go back.

Besides, I had already spent a vast amount of time and effort for Poland, and the Lord had enabled us to do something that, to my knowledge, had not been done for any other communist country in Europe: to print, ship, and distribute, with complete government sanction, thousands of *Illustrated New Testaments*. What had happened was a dream that took years to bring to fruition. But if the Lord could work in Poland, why not in the Ukraine?

While I continued to mull over thoughts of the Ukraine, the Lord gave me another surprise: He showed me that His plans for Poland's *Illustrated New Testament* were still not over. . . .

The burly Polish official smiled warmly, strode toward me, and hugged me as if I were a long-lost relative. "Thank you very much for the books you've been providing for our country!"

I hadn't expected such overt enthusiasm and was taken aback. I had stopped for a brief visit with this official, as I often did when in Poland. But his obvious warmth made this meeting seem more like a friendly social call to an old friend than a courteous visit to a Polish official. As we chatted I asked, "What are the possibilities for future shipments of our *Illustrated New Testaments*? Should we keep bothering you for import permits for these books?"

He smiled. "I don't foresee any problems in getting the permits. You just keep on asking."

Once again the Polish government had given us a green light to continue our *Illustrated New Testament* project and had even done so with overtly friendly gestures.

As friends and I traversed the Polish countryside in early 1986, the Lord gave me yet another glimpse of the impact that this book is making on that country. . . .

"Stop! Let's take a picture of that horse and wagon!" My friends were excited to see the slow-moving old wooden wagon piled high with hay, with the Polish family members seated on the wagon as the horse plodded toward us along the highway. My friends pulled out their cameras and gestured to the family that they wanted to take a picture. The Polish couple smiled, nodded, and stopped the horse.

As my friends adjusted their cameras, I picked up an *Illustrated New Testament*. Once the picture-taking was over, I walked over to the family and greeted them in Polish. Then I held up the New Testament and asked, "Have any of you ever read this book?"

Everyone's face lit up when they saw it, but it was the mother, her eyes shining from a face framed in an old kerchief, who exclaimed, *"Zycie Jezusa Chrystusa I Dzieje Apostolskie! The Illustrated New Testament!* We've been searching *every-where* for this book! Where can we get it?"

My soul stirred as I saw her earnestness. The book had been introduced to the country only about a year and a half earlier. How had this Polish farming family, miles from most major cities, heard about it? How long had they been looking for it?

I marveled once again at God's timing as my friends and I, traveling through Poland, had just "happened" to meet this family on an old country highway. With great pleasure I handed them a copy of the book they had been aching to read. "Here. This is a gift for you."

By early 1986, nearly 150,000 copies of the *Illustrated New Testament* had been printed and delivered to Poland, and we had the assurance of being able to continue that outreach.

A few years earlier, the Lord had established our printing operation to the point where we had received requests to print various theological books for Eastern Europe. I was thrilled that our printing outreach could expand to serve the needs of other East European countries. To date we have printed several thousand of these books and have plans to continue production indefinitely. However, these plans hinge on the purchase of additional printing equipment. Our T. P. Miller is wearing out, and we will need more equipment if we are to be effective in expanding our outreach.

In addition to the need for theological books, some people in Eastern Europe are still waiting for their first Bible. In Poland, the country with which I am most familiar, most evangelicals own their own Bibles, but many Catholics have been waiting years for one. Like the evangelicals, the Catholics are limited in what they can print, and what is printed must be divided among thousands of churches. One priest told me that some of his parishioners have put in an order for a Bible, have actually paid for it, but have been waiting for three to five years. And if this is the situation in Poland, what must it be like in other communist countries? I am reminded of an old Russian man I met in Poland close to the Russian border on one of my early trips. . . .

Our old car bumped along the dusty dirt road. I felt very far from civilization, with only a few Polish villages scattered across our path. As I drove, I noticed an old man shuffling by the side of the road, so I stopped to talk to him. He had a thick, white moustache and beard and had jauntily perched a dark cap on his head. He must have been nearly eighty. As I greeted him, he answered me in Russian.

"Have you ever read the Bible? I asked.

He turned his large, sad eyes on me and nodded. "I had a Bible at one time, but it was taken from me."

I had a big Russian Bible in my car. Who better to give it to than this old man, who had obviously cherished the one he had had before? The two of us walked back to my car, where I reached in and rummaged through my things. Finally I found the Bible and thrust it into the old man's hands. "Here," I said, "this is a gift for you."

For a few seconds, nothing registered on the gnarled old face. He held the book reverently, running his fingers over the title imprinted on the cover. Then he looked up at me, his face a picture of absolute joy, and thanked me profusely. As I drove away, I watched him in my rearview mirror, clutching his precious gift.

An isolated incident from the faraway past? A story that wouldn't be common today? Hardly. In mid-1986 another incident reminded me that many Poles are still waiting for their first Bible. One of them was Leon, who told me in his home about his narrow escape from death forty years before.

At the age of nineteen Leon had been arrested by the German S.S. and accused of collaborating with prisoners who had escaped from a concentration camp near Lublin, Poland. He and all the men of his village had waited behind a barbed-wire fence for the awful moment when they, too, would be "freed"—through the smokestack of a crematorium. And then, miraculously, Leon escaped through a sewer pipe, and years later he narrated those harrowing events to me. . . .

The stench was overpowering as, with tears streaming down his cheeks, Leon clamped the wad of rags more firmly over his nose. Desperately he continued crawling, inching forward through the slime. His hands were bruised from obstacles he had met in the total blackness of the narrow pipe, and his knees were worn raw. In addition, the exhaustion brought on by days of meager rations, hard work, and mental torture gnawed at his stamina. Never in his nineteen years had he felt more miserable. The sewer pipe seemed to go on forever. Would he be able to make it through? He couldn't remember ever feeling so utterly alone. "Oh, God!" he breathed. "I'm too young to die! Help me! Oh, please, help me!"

As he struggled to move, muscles aching and teeth chattering, Leon tried to focus his eyes straight ahead of him in the darkness. Suddenly he stopped and squinted. Was it—could it be—a shaft of light? Mustering what strength he could, he pushed toward it. Steadily it grew larger until Leon finally realized that it was the end of the pipe. Minutes later he emerged—filthy, cramped and bleeding, but free at last.

Now, four decades later, I was in Leon's house and listening to his story. I asked, "Have you ever wondered why God spared you from that crematorium?

Leon sighed and stared down at the table.

"I think I know," I added gently. "In order that you might hear God's message of love and salvation." I pulled a Polish New Testament from my pocket. "Have you ever read this?"

He looked at it and shook his head. "No. I've never seen a Bible in my life."

I smiled. Joy welling up within me, I handed sixty-year-old Leon his first portion of Scripture.

Opportunities to preach . . . a hunched old woman asking for a tract . . . children running excitedly beside the mobile chapel . . . a young artist who had never before seen a New Testament . . . "nonskid eternal soles, guaranteed for 10,000 miles" . . . the provision of a T. P. Miller offset press . . . 150,000 copies of the *Polish Illustrated New Testament* . . . "I'll give you all the money I have for that Bible" . . . the sorrow on Polish orphans' faces turning to joy . . . "Could you preach again?" . . . the broken alabster box . . . "All of Poland is asking for that book."

For over thirty years, the joys and trials, triumphs and heartaches, provisions and needs of Eastern Europe have been my own. I can scarcely draw a breath without thinking of the people who have become dearer than life itself.

And now, as the Lord continues to open doors, as He places new vistas before me and assures me that some of my old dreams will continue, I dare to dream new dreams—for Poland, for the Ukraine, and for the rest of Eastern Europe.

If you would like more information about the ministry of Bill Kapitaniuk, write:

> Bill Kapitaniuk
> Slavic Gospel Association
> P.O. Box 1122
> Wheaton, IL 60189